FAST, CLEAN AND CHEAP

or EVERYTHING the Jewish teacher (or parent) needs to know about ART

by Simon Kops
edited by Carolyn Moore Mooso

RATNER MEDIA AND TECHNOLOGY CENTER
JEWISH EDUCATION CENTER OF CLEVELAND

TORAH AURA PRODUCTIONS
LOS ANGELES, CALIFORNIA

ISBN # 0-933873-25-5

Library of Congress Catalog-in-Publication Data

Kops, Simon, 1921-
  Fast, clean, and cheap : or everything the Jewish teacher and parent needs to know about art / by Simon Kops.
   p. cm.
   ISBN 0-933873-25-5
   1. Activity programs in Jewish religious education. 2. Judaism—Study and teaching (Primary) I. Title.
BM103.K66 1988
296.6'8—dc19   88-20109
                                            CIP

Material for introductions first appeared in
Liturgical Arts Volume 1, Issue 1, May 1985.
Ecumenical Liturgical Arts Guild
3217 Center Avenue
Madison, Wisconsin 53704
and in
Bikurim, a publication of the Coalition for the Advancement of
Jewish Education.

© 1989 Simon Kops
Published by Torah Aura Productions
All rights reserved. No part of this publication may be reproduced or transmitted in any form or by any means graphic, electronic or mechanical including photocopying, recording or by any information storage and retrieval system, without permission in writing from the publisher.
Torah Aura Productions
4423 Fruitland Avenue
Los Angeles, CA 90058

MANUFACTURED IN THE UNITED STATES OF AMERICA

To Deborah and Lise
to Elad, Maya and Lila
and to all the children in the world

CONTENTS

PREFACE 7
GETTING STARTED: BASIC TOOLS AND MATERIALS 8

THE "MAGIC" OF JEWISH EDUCATION: ILLUSIONS AND PAPER FOLDS TO ENLIVEN YOUR TEACHING 11
    The Lulav 12
    The Religious Marriage 14
    Jacob's Ladder 15
    The Magic Blackboard 16
    Growing Religion (Moebius strip) 17
    Twelve Tribes, United 18
    Parting of the Red Sea 19
    Unbreakable Judaism 20
    Which Is Bigger? (Optical illusion) 21
    Singular and Plural 22

SOME VERSATILE TECHNIQUES (AND SAMPLE CLASSROOM PROJECTS) 23
The Collage 24
    Joseph's coat 24
    Jerusalem skyline #1 26
    Jerusalem skyline #2 27
    Imitation Stained Glass 28
Some Simple Help To Make Drawing People Easier 29
Origami (Paper-folding) 30
    Paper napkin flower 30
    Star of David 31
    Hamantaschen candy dish 32
Copper repousse 33
    Mizrah 34
    Mezuzah 36
    Pendant 37
Clay projects 38
    Tablets of the Law 39
    Western Wall 40
Bingo games 41
    Aleph Bet bingo 41
    Twelve tribe bingo 42
Follow the dots 44
    Alef 44
    Dreidel 45
    Menorah 45
    Torah 45
Edible Judaism 46

SOME WAYS TO ADD PEP TO "PLAIN OLD PICTURES" 47
A pull-apart picture 48
Magical, mystical chalk picture 49
Starburst designs 50

Fast, Clean & Cheap

Contrast designs 51
Paper chain wall decoration 52
MORE CLASSROOM PROJECTS 53
Paper kippah 54
Three-dimensional paper animals 55
Double name contour drawing 56
Multi-design Hebrew name 57
Judaic wind sock 58
Seder plate 59
Matzah cover 60
Kiddush cup (Elijah's Cup) 61
Drinking-straw dreidel 62
Pin the Shamash on the Hanukkiah 63
Star of David
    1) Magic triangle 64
    2) Drinking-straw (linear) star 65
    3) A one-cut Star of David 66
    4) Magen David pinwheel 67
    5) Magen David streamers 68
Shabbat mats 69
New Year cards
    1) French fold card 70
    2) Folded 3-D star card 71
    3) Ark and Torah card 72
    4) Honeycomb card 73
Some costume accessories
    1) Crown 74
    2) Paper domino mask 75
    3) Paper bag mask 76
    4) Egg carton mask 77
    5) Three-cornered hat 78
Purim Gragger 79
Stencilled paper Israeli flag 80
Lacing card Israeli flag 81
Flowers
    Tissue paper flowers 82
    A simple flower bouquet 83
    Flower basket 84
Refrigerator magnets 85
Paper Hanukkah lantern 86
Wooden Hanukkiah 87
Judaic memory box 88

Glossary 89
List of Suppliers 90

Preface

After 35 years of teaching art, and 20 years of teaching religious school, it was inevitable that I would evolve the theory of "Fast, Clean and Cheap," for more effective religious school teaching through visual (art) experiences.

Attempts to incorporate art experiences into religious school teaching are beset with obstacles. Often, recalcitrant students would rather be elsewhere. The time allotted is insufficient for intended projects. Storage space is usually nonexistent. Multi-purpose rooms may be carpeted or furnished so as to preclude the use of clay, plaster or paint. Budgets of religious schools are notoriously meager. However, despite these and other difficulties, a religious school program that emphasizes visual aspects *can* be implemented.

Why Emphasize the Visual?

My reasons for this emphasis are three. First, since very young students have little or no reading skill, the visual approach is one of the main teaching avenues that exists. Secondly, for those who can read, art provides experiential enrichment to augment texts and other kinds of learning activities. Finally, with an art project to clutch (and take home), the student has a tangible manifestation of what has been taught and learned, however abstract the basic concept may be.

In addition, every group of learners exhibits a variety of learning styles. Some students learn what they hear, while others can learn only what they see; some absorb what they read, but others take in only what they can touch. Effective teachers are distinguished by their attention to such differences. They make every effort to include in their lessons activities that accomodate all learning styles, and hands-on art projects are a staple item in their classes for this reason.

Fast/Clean/Cheap/Safe

Within this visual approach, it is most effective to utilize techniques that are:

FAST—Because time is of the essence.

CLEAN—Because the maintenance staff will love you, and they are valuable allies.

CHEAP—Because your administrator will love you.

To the above criteria, also add

SAFE—Because some materials and procedures are definitely hazardous and should be avoided.

I remarked earlier that I think my long experience in teaching led inevitably to my conclusions about what kinds of art projects work best. Thus, it is no surprise that a great many other experienced teachers have also determined that an art project for a religious school class needs to be **FAST, CLEAN** and **CHEAP**. Unfortunately, too many have also concluded—often after surveying a disappointing supply cabinet—that the only available art experience that meets these criteria is drawing with crayons. It need not be so—and that is the reason for this book.

Fast, Clean & Cheap

Getting Started: Basic Tools and Materials

Every successful art program has two basic kinds of components, the concrete (tools and materials) and the abstract (ideas, skills and techniques). I'll begin by recommending some basic necessities (and a few exciting frills) that fall into the first category.

Tools and Equipment Every School Needs

Pantograph. Not all teachers are art teachers, and very few are graphic artists. One of the most helpful items for teachers who don't draw skilfully is the pantograph, a tool consisting of several wood or metal strips connected by pivoting joints that can be used to copy, enlarge, or reduce drawings and diagrams. A pantograph costs about $12.00, and is a one-time investment that pays for itself in the time saved. The teachers' time (whether paid or unpaid) is probably the most expensive commodity involved in religious school.

Scissors *for Students*. There are many types of scissors on the market now. For the very young, there are training scissors, with finger holes for the teacher as well as the student. Some shears have springs so that they will revert to the open position. Remember that not every student is right-handed. It is extremely frustrating for a left-handed student to cut with right-handed shears. In addition to left-handed shears (which are marked as such on the blade), there are some new plastic shears on the market that can be used with either hand.

Special Scissors *for Teachers*. Serrated scissors, leather shears and polyester double-knit shears have serrated blades, so that several layers of paper an be cut together without sliding. They also minimize the force needed to cut.
Pinking shears are also nice to have on hand. These cut a zigzag edge that helps to prevent fabric from ravelling and creates an additional decorative effect when cutting paper for some uses, such as when making paper flowers.

Razor Blades. A single-edged razor blade or a mat knife with replaceable blades is good for cutting cardboard and heavy paper, or many layers of ordinary paper at once. When cutting, always work on a stack of newspapers to protect both the blade and the surface underneath. Razor blades and mat knives are very useful to the teacher, but should **never** be given to the students to use. **Stapler.** A stapler or a staple gun can be used for bulletin boards and constructions. A clipper-type stapler is handy for fastening things; this can be used with one hand.

Paper punch.

Stencils. Stencils are inexpensive tools for many projects. Cut a stencil of the object to be reproduced out of good quality tagboard (a mat knife comes in handy here). A good stencil will last for hundreds of copies. Make masking tape tabs on the stencil to lift the stencil after each use—it saves paint on the fingers. To use the stencil, place it on poster or construction paper. Using a can of spray paint (silver and gold work best, as they have the least amount of residue), spray LIGHTLY so that the outline is evident. **NEVER** spray indoors. A large cardboard carton can be used as a makeshift spray booth. Use these stencils for coloring, collage outlines, cut-outs, etc.

Basic Supplies and Materials for Art Projects

Adhesives. My favorite form of adhesive is the old standard library paste. It is safe, it is easily available, it washes out of clothing, and it is inexpensive. Many people avoid it because of ineffective adhesion which is the result of improper usage. To use it correctly, apply a small amount of paste to EACH of the two surfaces to be joined, RUB until the surfaces become shiny, and then put the two surfaces together. Joined this way, they will never come apart. Another cheap and relatively clean adhesive is liquid laundry starch, which is sold in gallon or half-gallon bottles in grocery and variety stores. It works well for attaching lightweight paper to a firmer background. Most other popular adhesives fall short of one or more of the criteria we want to meet—**FAST, CLEAN, CHEAP,** and **SAFE**. Rubber cement is one example. Most of us are aware of the toxic fumes from many quick-drying airplane glues. Not many are aware of a far more insidious poison in rubber cement. Children love to play with it, yet the solvent used in rubber cement can be toxic to a 180-pound adult. Think what it can do to a 40-pound child! Casein glues, also called "white glue", can be disastrous to clothing, carpet and upholstery, although they can be cleaned up with water while still wet. This type of glue is also messy when used by children because it is liquid and therefore harder to control than paste. Recently, though, a water soluble casein glue that can be washed out of clothing has come on the market. It might be worthwhile to try to locate this type for the occasional project that requires a casein glue. (There are a few such projects in this book.)

Coloring and Drawing Materials. Oil crayons are beautiful, but play havoc with carpeting. Markers give good strong color—but be sure that the markers are water soluble. If the marker has a solvent odor, avoid it at all costs. Colored pencils give good results, but have a more limited area of coverage. They are good for older students. The old standby, the wax crayon, is still the cheapest and the best. Crayons can also be used on fabric, and ironed for permanency. Crayon stubs can be melted together to make multicolored crayon pieces (terrific for rainbow effects, such as Noah's Ark).

Tape. Be aware of the various types of tape on the market. Cellulose (Scotch) tape is designed for one-time application. It is not good for mounting pictures, since it doesn't "give" with the humidity. Masking tape is much better; it can also be repositioned. Cloth or vinyl sticky tape is strong and comes in colors for easy collage projects, but is relatively expensive.

Paper. Ubiquitous paper, the foundation of most art projects, is available in many forms. It may be poetic justice that paper, which had its origin in the papyrus of ancient Egypt, can now be used to illustrate Biblical events like th Exodus. The teacher should be aware that different papers have different qualities and are NOT interchangeable. Tissue paper is of very light weight and limp. It is good for flowers and items that need to be molded by crushing. Bond paper and construction paper are stiff—best used for folded projects. Don't forget to score fold lines for a crisp folded edge. Paper towels and napkins are very fibrous and will stretch a bit, but have no inherent strength. Cardboards, tagboards, bristol boards, pasteboards, illustration boards, etc., are great for construction projects. They usually can be cut best with a mat knife rather than scissors.

Bear in mind that most paper and boards will fade in sunlight. Fadeless papers can be purchased, but at a premium price. It's best to plan paper use carefully for economy's sake, so that projects are sized to use paper efficiently. Most papers come in sizes that are multiples of 9 x 12 inches.

Some Special Materials That Add Spice

Our students today live in a very visually stimulating environment. They are constantly bombarded with sophisticated visual imagery. Commonplace materials—pencil, newsprint, paper—are old hat. They look for sophistication. Luckily, there are many new materials on the market (as well as some that have always been there but are unfamiliar) that will delight them. A few examples follow, but you should be on the lookout for others.

Honeycomb paper. The honeycomb paper found in old valentines is now available by the sheet. Although expensive per sheet, it can be cut into "bite-size" pieces for maximum utilization. The three-dimensional effect makes impressive decorations and greeting cards.

Sequins and Glitter. All children love to embellish with sequins. Don't buy them at a fabric store; they're too expensive that way. Buy them at an art supply house. At approximately $10.00 per pound, you will bring excitement to your classes for over a year. Glitter has a similarly enticing effect, but is more likely to be messy. Both glitter and sequins are neater to work with if the whole project can be confined within a shallow gift-box lid.

Metallic pens. These come in thick and thin widths. Available in solid metallics or with an outline of gold or silver around another color, they are another source of joy.

Sheet Metal and Metal foils. Aluminum foil is an old standby that adds sparkle to many projects, but thin sheet metal is also within the reach of most budgets (at least for small projects) and gives students the sense that they are creating a durable, permanent keepsake or gift.

Recyclables. There is a windfall for teachers and students in the competitive marketplace that leads to increasingly flashy and elaborate packaging of all kinds of products. Cardboard tubes and egg cartons are versatile and easy to obtain, but there are also wonderful possibilities in various styrofoam packing materials, containers with interesting shapes, and boxes made of clear acetate or coated with foil or Mylar.
One classic example is the egg-shaped plastic boxes that encapsulate one brand of pantyhose, which come in various colors and sit in a stiff cardboard collar that holds them upright.

Where Can I Find These Things?

The question arises "Where do I find these materials?" You can find some at art or stationery stores or in catalogs. Although these catalogs are usually sold for about $3.00, they are often sent free if requested on school stationery. These will not only tell you what is available, but also give you some ideas. Remember, though, that some items, such as spray paint, can be purchased more cheaply at local hardware or discount stores. A list of some possible suppliers appears in an appendix at the end of this book.

Don't overlook parents as resource people. Daddy's factory may have rejects of paper tubes, leather scraps, yarn, etc., while Mom's interior design studio probably discards carpet, fabric and wallpaper samples on a regular basis. You can also be pretty sure that, in any given class, one or more parents can provide you with an endless supply of waste computer paper from home or office. This paper is ususally firm and lightweight, fine for sketching and paper-folding projects. Parents can also be enlisted to collect household recyclables like scraps of wood or fabric and various packaging materials like egg cartons, paper towel tubes, baby food jars, empty spools, or the aforementioned "eggs". We do live in a disposable society, and finding ways to use such items cuts down on general waste as well as providing cost-free materials for art projects.

What has been presented here is only a brief guide and outline. When it comes to art materials and tools, the heavens are truly the limit. Applying the standards discussed above—**FAST, CLEAN, CHEAP** and **SAFE**—can help you choose the ones that will best meet your needs and those of your students.

THE "MAGIC" OF JEWISH EDUCATION: ILLUSIONS AND PAPER FOLDS TO ENLIVEN YOUR TEACHING

While most of this book is filled with ideas and projects intended to help you provide "hands-on" art experiences for your students, you as the teacher can provide visual reinforcement of your lesson all by yourself, creating illusions and illustrations that will add impact to your teaching.

The art of magic dates back to pre-biblical times. People have always liked to be mystified, baffled and entertained. If education can be pursued in the guise of entertainment, the struggle becomes much easier. The student's antipathy is converted to interest with a minimum of effort. The student is left with a sense of wonderment that is a good foundation for future learning. This is especially pertinent to religious studies, which can be intangible and are usually non-visual.

The following phenomena (rather than calling them "tricks") require a bare minimum of dexterity on the part of the teacher. Rather, they rely on physical properties, attractions and conditions. The phenomena can be used as illustrations or adjuncts to various appropriate stories, depending upon curriculum, students' ages and comprehension, and available time. All require simple materials, which make the results seem even more spectacular to the student. Some tricks can be repeated over and over. Others are one-time occurrences. For those that require some deception, do *not* reveal the secret. Remember, your students do have younger brothers and sisters who would also like to be amazed. Leaving them in wonderment boosts your rating as an educator who can do anything and everything. Some of the following exercises have been staples of night club and TV performers. I have tried to place them within the context of religious education, and you will undoubtedly find other ways in which to do so.

The Lulav

Materials needed: 2 double sheets large-size newspaper (want ads are best)

Cut or tear apart the newspaper, horizontally. This will give you four parts, which you can name for the four species that are needed for the celebration of SUKKOT. Pass out the sections with a name for each—THE ETROG, THE WILLOW, THE MYRTLE, and THE PALM. Take one section, calling out its name, and roll it into a tube about 1 1/2 inches in diameter. Take the second strip, again calling out its name, and continue rolling, overlapping the end of the second strip about 5 inches within the first. Continue to roll in this fashion, and add the last two strips. Remember, this is a learning exercise as well as a magic trick. As you roll, discuss the symbols that the strips of newpaper represent.

Squeeze and flatten the tube (#1). Tear the layers of the tube halfway down (#2). Squeeze in opposite direction (#3). Tear again halfway down. This will give you a tube with the upper part divided into four sections.

Pinch back section at the base of the tear.

Now say the proper blessing for the Lulav.

Gripping the bottom (not too tightly), slowly pull the innermost torn strip. The Lulav can be pulled to a height of about 5 feet. Prolong the wonderment by pulling it out slowly. With younger students this can be done over and over again. Practice first to get the proper tension for the rolling. If tearing is too difficult the tube may be cut, but tearing produces a better effect.

Squeeze.

Tear halfway down.

Squeeze in other direction and tear halfway down.

Pinch.

Pull.

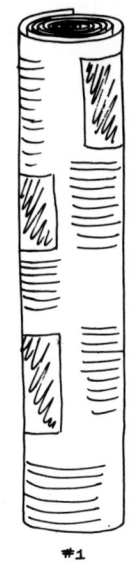
#1

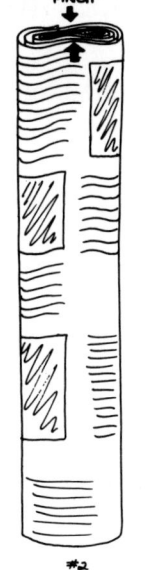
#2

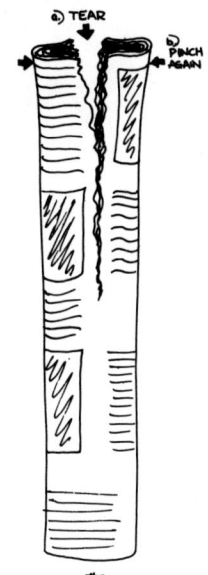
#3

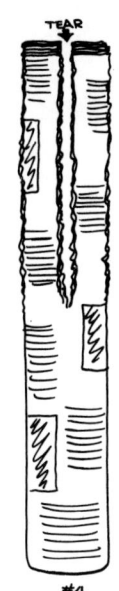
#4

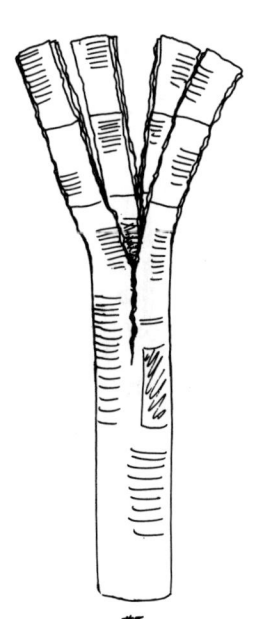
#5

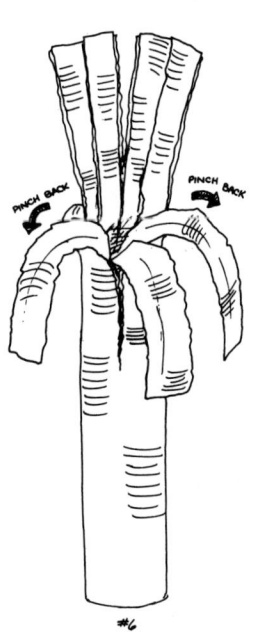
#6

#7

Fast, Clean & Cheap

The Religious Marriage

Materials needed: 2 paper clips of equal size
a strip of paper about 1" x 12"

This is a good way to illustrate the uniting of two disparate entities, joined together by a common bond. For example, the two entities, male and female, are joined by a religious marriage to make a union. You could also use it to illustrate STUDY and CHARITY joined by the TORAH, or JACOB and ESAU, joined by BROTHERHOOD. The possibilities are endless. Tailor them to your curriculum.

Loop the paper into a compressed "S" shape. Place the paper clips as indicated in the diagram (where ends meet the rounded portions of the "S"). Push the paper clips all the way down. Slowly, pull the ends of the strip apart. The clips will magically unite. While doing this, talk about the meaning of union as oneness. This can be repeated over and over. It always works.

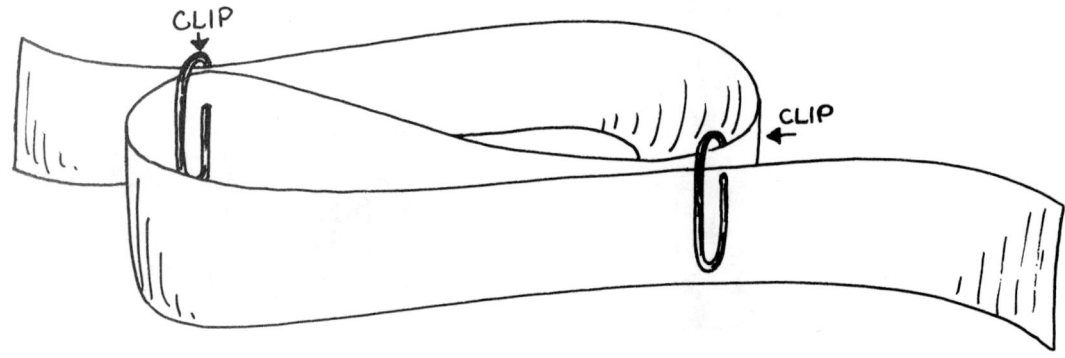

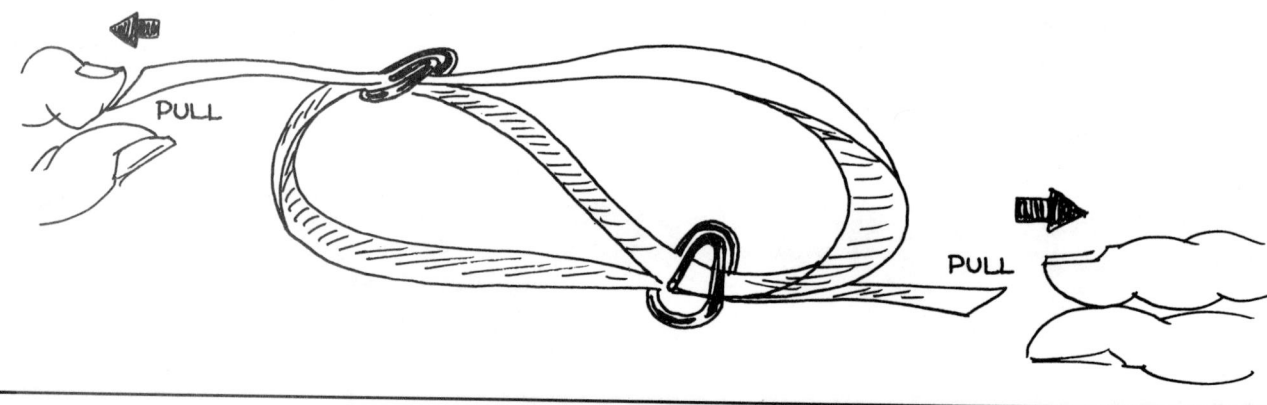

Jacob's Ladder

Materials needed: One large double sheet of newspaper (not the tabloid size)
sharp scissors

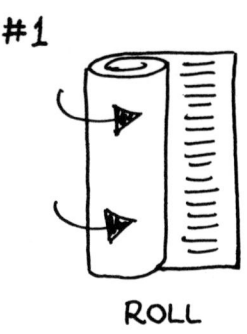
ROLL

This illustrates an occurrence during Jacob's wandering in the desert. Students should already know or should be told the background story of the twins, Jacob and Esau—one a hunter, the other a farmer. Esau, the older, sold his birthright to Jacob for a "mess of pottage". With older students, this is a good place to dwell on the meaning of birthright and inheritance as contrasted with today's customs.

Tear or cut the newspaper horizontally so that you have two long, narrow strips. These two strips might represent Jacob and Esau, or birthright and inheritance. Roll one strip so that it forms a tube with a diameter of about 1 1/2 inches. Overlap the next piece about 5 inches putting the end of the second strip underneath the first. From the center section of the resulting tube, cut out a piece about 3 inches long, leaving a strip about 1/2 inch by 3 inches connecting the two end tubes—all the while talking about the story, up to the point where Jacob flees. Fold back the two end tubes. At the climactic moment, when Jacob is asleep with his head on a rock, dreaming of angels going up and down between himself and heaven, pull the center strip carefully. Lo and behold, there is the ladder for the angels to travel on. Practice this several times to get the right tightness and tension in your paper roll.

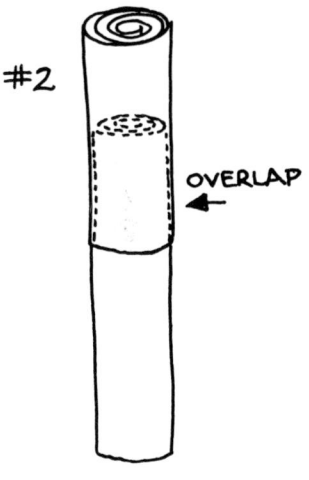
OVERLAP

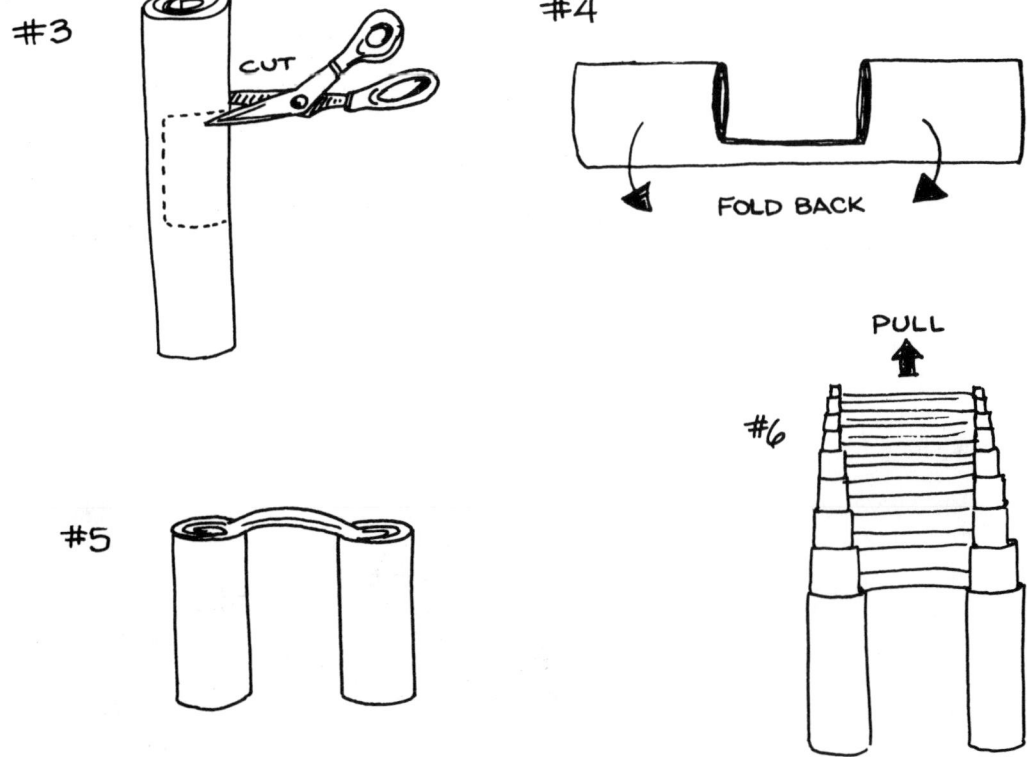

Fast, Clean & Cheap 15

The Magic Blackboard

Materials needed: chalkboard
chalk
wet sponge or paper towel

When the students enter the room, they find a list of loosely connected words on the blackboard, such as STUDY, HONESTY, CHARITY, TORAH, WISDOM and RESPECT.

Lead a class discussion as to which is most important, without reaching a conclusion. Then call on the most argumentative or most doubtful student to erase the board evenly. Lo and behold, all words are erased but TORAH. The students are mystified. This can be applied to any lesson in which you wish to highlight a particular word, name or concept.

The secret is easy. Before the students arrive, wet a portion of the board with a sponge or paper towel. While the board is wet, write in the wet area the word(s) you want to emphasize. When the board has dried add any other words or drawings you wish. The wetness bonds the chalk to the board, making it difficult to erase. The chalkboard is not ruined. All can be removed with a wet sponge. Do not disclose the secret. Keeping the students mystified will heighten their interest.

Growing Religion (Moebius strip)

Materials needed: paper strip about 2" x 24"
scissors
paste

Make a loop of the paper strip, making one turn in the paper before pasting the ends together. Talk about the hostile forces which, through the ages, have attempted to divide the Jewish religion—all the while cutting the paper strip lengthwise through the middle. When the cut (and the story) is completely finished, the strip is not in two pieces, but still in one piece, and larger than before. Thus, sometimes, religion grows stronger in adversity.

The phenomenon is known in mathematics as the Moebius strip. If the strip is not twisted, you get two separate strips. Twisted once, you get one larger strip. Twisted twice, you get two interlocking strips. These other variations may be used to illustrate other stories. With the strip at least 24 inches long, the twists are not apparent. Gummed sealing tape is excellent for this.

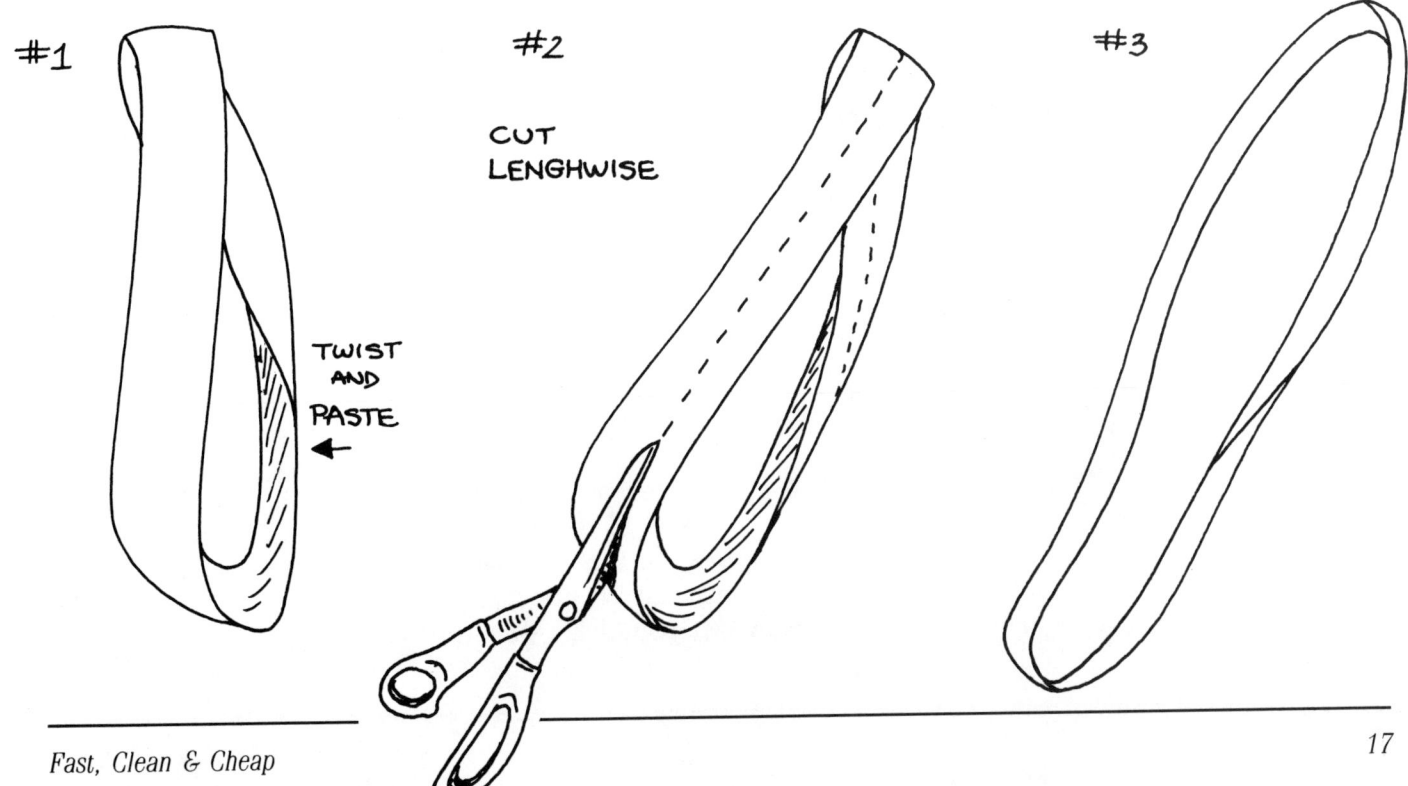

Fast, Clean & Cheap

Twelve Tribes, United

Materials Needed: 24 paper clips
envelope
glue

Twelve paper clips are passed out. These represent the twelve tribes. You can discuss the order of the tribes, what each tribe was noted for, what the symbol of each tribe was, etc. The 12 individual clips are collected and put into an envelope, one by one. The envelope is sealed. The envelope is shaken to prove that they are within. Leaving the envelope in plain sight, discuss what would be a unifying force to make these 12 tribes into a nation. Would it be MOSES, the EXODUS, CANAAN, STATEHOOD, or what? When the class decides, write the answer on the envelope. With a great flourish, tear one end of the envelope, and the paper clips emerge linked together—UNITED.

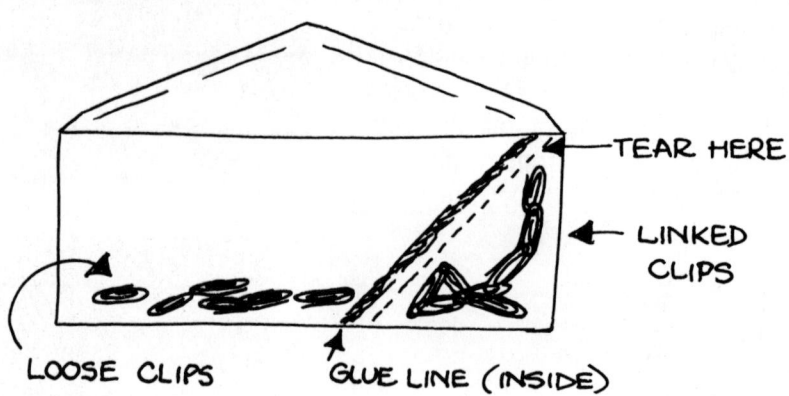

This requires a bit of preparation. In advance of the class, link 12 clips together and push to one side of the envelope. Glue that part of the envelope (see diagram). When the glue has dried, the inside of the envelope can be shown empty—and the illusion can proceed. After presenting the illusion, discard the envelope quickly—and proceed with the lesson.

Parting of the Red Sea

Materials needed: clean dinner plate (preferably white)
water
ordinary black ground pepper
soap (liquid soap works best)

For Passover, this is an impressive visual effect that will firmly embed itself in the minds of the onlookers.

Depending upon the age and curriculum of the students, tell an appropriate version of the story of the sojourn in Egypt, starting with Joseph and ending with Moses leading the Israelites out of Egypt. When you come to the climactic moment when the Hebrews reach the Red Sea, with the Egyptians in hostile pursuit, fill the dinner plate with clean water.

Sprinkle black pepper on the water to simulate the "Red" sea. (Red pepper or paprika do not work quite as well). At the point in the story when the Hebrews are sandwiched between the sea and the Egyptians, Moses reaches out, touches the water, and the water (pepper) parts. The effect is mystifying.

The "secret" is that some soap is hidden under your fingernail. If you can manage it surreptitiously, liquid soap works even better. When your finger touches the water, the soap alters the surface tension of the water, and the pepper miraculously parts. Students will try this but the pepper will not part. However, you will not be able to make it part again either; this can only be done once each time it is set up.

Do not reveal the soap secret—your stature will increase.

Fast, Clean & Cheap

Unbreakable Judaism

Materials needed: a clean white handerkerchief with a hem
2 toothpicks

A clean white handkerchief is shown to the students. It is not passed around. Instead, it is held aloft by one corner, reversed, shaken, etc., so that the students can see that nothing is hidden. An ordinary toothpick is shown to the students—it can be passed around and even marked, so that the students know that nothing has been substituted. The toothpick represents Judaism. If you squeeze the toothpick in the middle, nothing is broken. If you bend the toothpick it breaks. Thus, the fragile nature of religion.

The marked toothpick is placed in the middle of the handkerchief. The handkerchief is crumpled. Allow a student (the biggest doubter in the class) to feel the toothpick through the cloth, and bend and break it. Still holding onto the cloth, let others feel the break or perhaps add new breaks. Next, deliver the appropriate lecture on the fragility of religion. The cloth is opened, shaken out, and the toothpick is whole. It can be passed around the room to validate the wholeness. AMAZEMENT.

The secret is to use a handkerchief with a hem. A toothpick is secretly hidden in the hem. This is the toothpick that is broken. Carefully, wad the handkerchief so that the hem toothpick is offered and broken while the loose toothpick is protected. The handkerchief can be held and shaken by one corner to prove that is empty. Nonchalantly put the kerchief in your pocket while attention is focused on the "unbreakable" toothpick. A little practice helps on this.

Optical Illusion—
Which is Bigger?

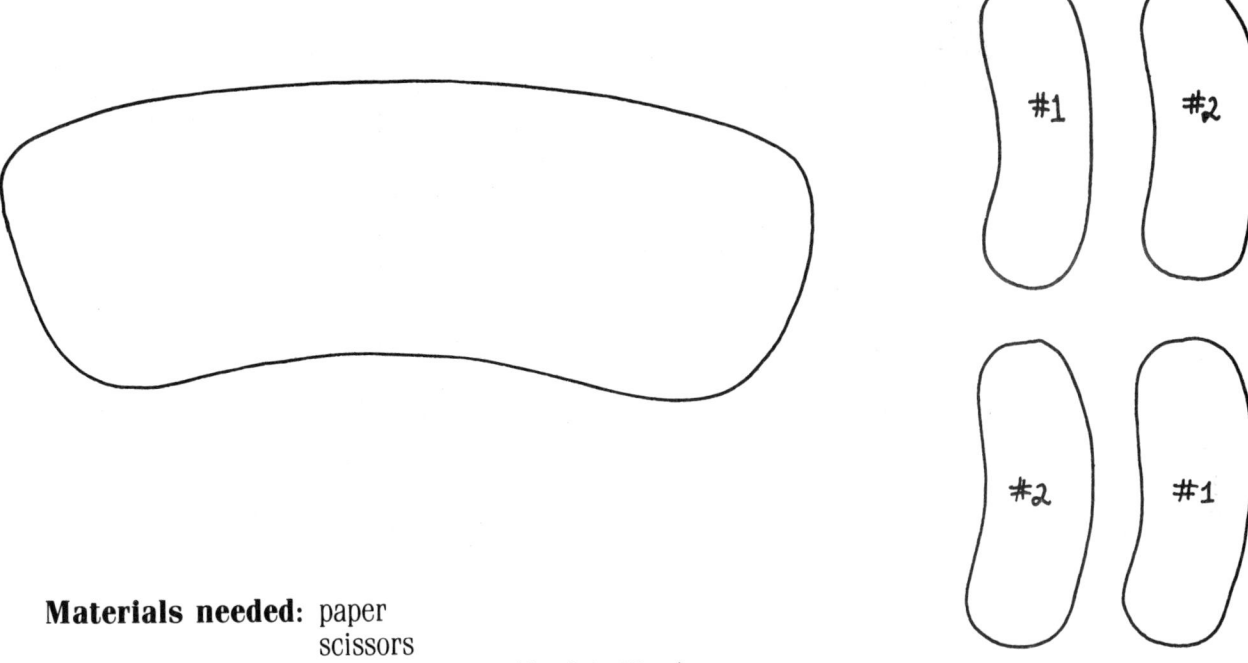

Materials needed: paper
scissors
pen or marker (for labelling)

Cut TWO identical shapes as indicated in the diagram. Depending upon your curriculum, pick two values, virtues, sins, events, personalities or prayers that you want your students to compare and argue about in terms of their relative value or significance. Some sample pairs might be:

Study of Torah	Mitzvot
Tzedakah	Prayer
Abraham	Moses
David	Samuel
Shema	Kaddish
Honesty	Kindness
Stealing	Lying
Holocaust	Destruction of the Temple

Label the pieces with the two things you want the class to discuss and argue about. The piece on the left will appear larger, hence more important. Let the discussion proceed for awhile with this "illustration" before the class. Then reverse the pieces—now the new piece on the left will appear larger. This should occasion some new arguments. This is an optical illusion. Both pieces are identical. To make sure that this is so, cut them out together from a folded piece of paper.

Fast, Clean & Cheap

Singular and Plural

Materials needed: a strip of thin paper about 3" x 24" (tissue or newsprint are good for this) scissors

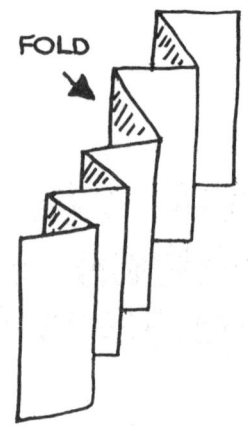

This is a visual illustration, rather than a trick.

Fold the long, narrow strip of paper back and forth, accordion-style, so that the resulting shape is a rectangle about the size of a business card.

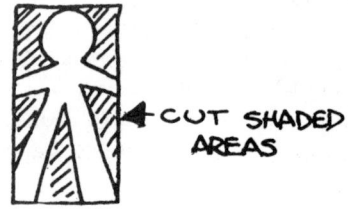

Then make a simple cut-out, a boy for example, remembering to leave some part—hands and feet in this example—connected at the edges. The still-folded papercut is shown to the students as the appropriate singular word (in this case "yeled," meaning boy) is spoken and possibly written on the board. Then, presto, chango—the paper is unfolded, and "yeled" (boy) becomes the plural—"yeladim" (boys).

This simple technique works well for any words with visual images—girl, star, flower, dog, etc.

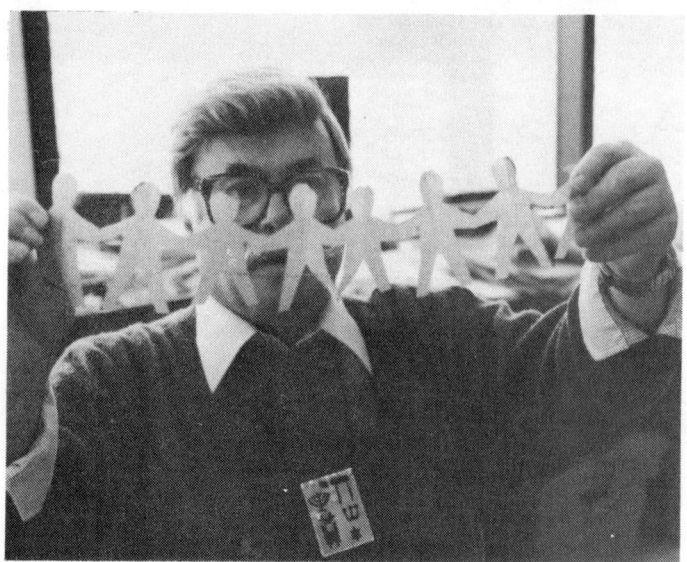

Fast, Clean & Cheap

SOME VERSATILE TECHNIQUES AND SAMPLE CLASSROOM PROJECTS

The last section described some ways that you, the teacher (or parent), might use some **FAST, CLEAN** and **CHEAP** materials for "special effects" to enhance your teaching. Now we move on to some general techniques for classroom (or home) art projects that meet those same criteria and are endlessly versatile. While some sample projects using each of these techniques are described in detail, the techniques and materials themselves can be adapted to any subject matter and used in a wide variety of applications. Use your imagination, and you'll discover that the sample projects described are only the tip of the iceberg.

Collages

A collage (from the French word, *coller*, to paste) is a quick, easy method of injecting color, shape and texture into a two-dimensional drawing that otherwise might be flat and lifeless. White casein glues are adequate, but they are expensive and could be injurious to clothing. They are also hard to clean up, once they have dried. A better, cheaper, safer substitute for the glue is undiluted liquid laundry starch. Supermarkets sell generic brands in gallon or half-gallon sizes. This works perfectly and is cheap. Dispense small quantities in souffle cups. Give students either bristle or foam brushes. Even if starch dries in the brushes, they can be reclaimed with warm water. For pasting, use starch undiluted as it comes from the container.

Collage #1—Joseph's Coat

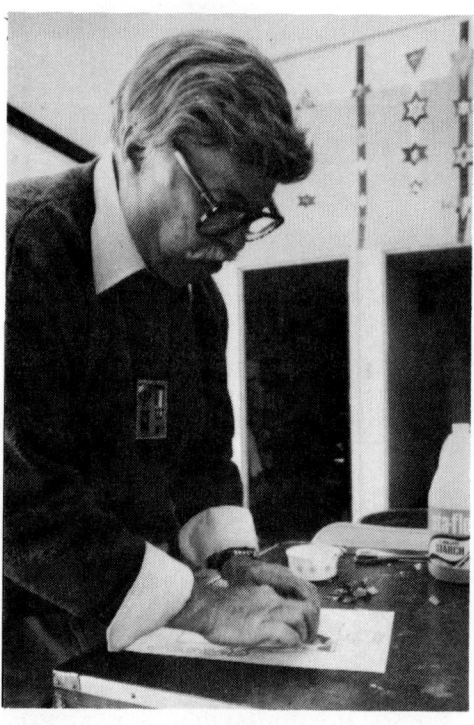 

Materials needed: laundry starch
brushes
copies of outline picture of Joseph (one per student)
paper and fabric scraps, sequins
scissors

Paint the areas of Joseph's coat with the starch. Give students scraps of colored tissue, lightweight cloth scraps, bits of colored paper and, as an extra treat, a handful of sequins. Press down all of the decorative materials. Excess starch that may come up can easily be washed off with warm water.

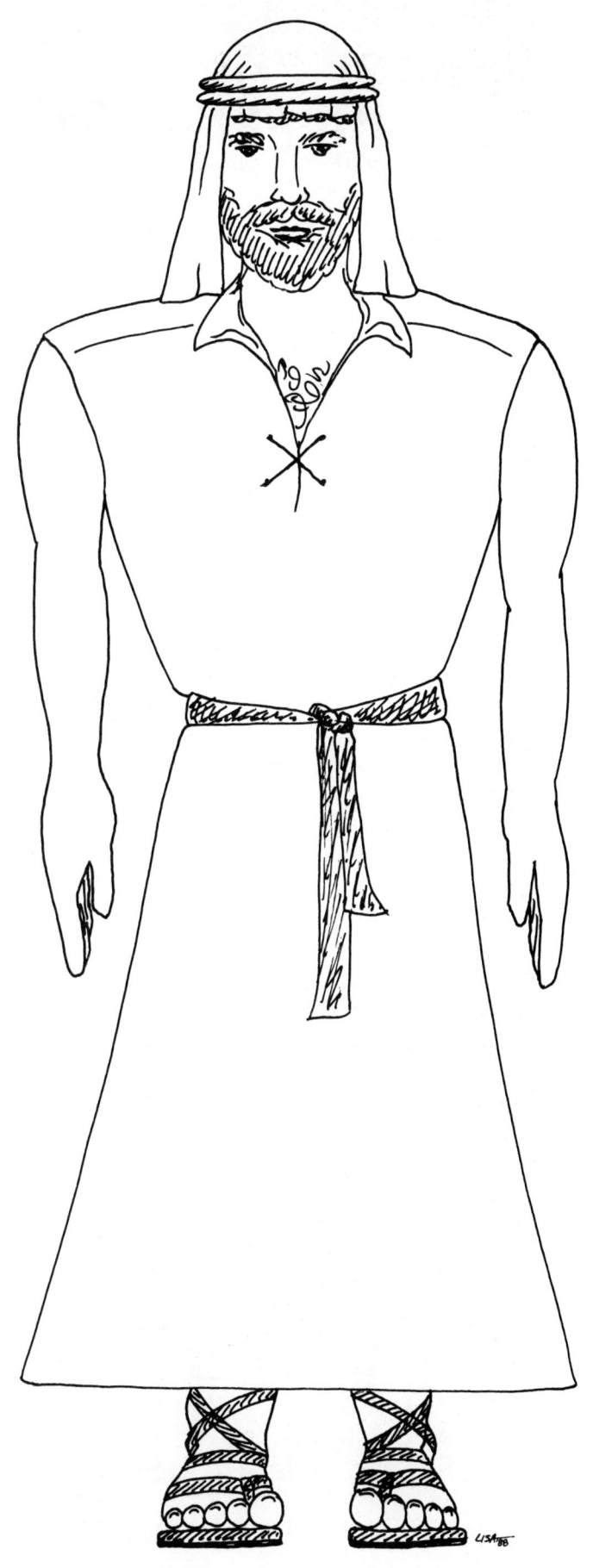

Collage #2—
Jerusalem Skyline #1

Materials needed: laundry starch
brushes
precut colored tissue paper shapes
heavy paper, tagboard or railroad board

From assorted colors of tissue paper, precut assorted simple geometric shapes (squares, triangles, circles, semicircles, rectangles, etc.). Have the students coat backround paper (tagboard or railroad board works best) with a heavy layer of undiluted laundry starch. Arrange shapes to form a skyline. Encourage overlapping, as this will create new forms *and* new colors. Allow to dry before stacking. The excess starch will give a shiny "shellacked" surface, which will enhance the picture's effectiveness.

Collage #3— Jerusalem Skyline #2

Materials needed: laundry starch
brushes
tagboard
construction paper
metallic paper
sequins
scissors
crayons or markers

Use the same procedures as in collage #2, but this time, use colored construction paper for the assorted shapes. Older students might want to cut their own shapes and forms. Add SMALL pieces of colored metallic paper and a few sequins. Students love metallics and sequins. When thoroughly dry, use crayons or markers to add details such as doors, windows, minarets, etc. Despite the similarity in technique, the different materials create a completely different effect from the tissue-paper skyline collage.

Collage #4— Imitation Stained Glass

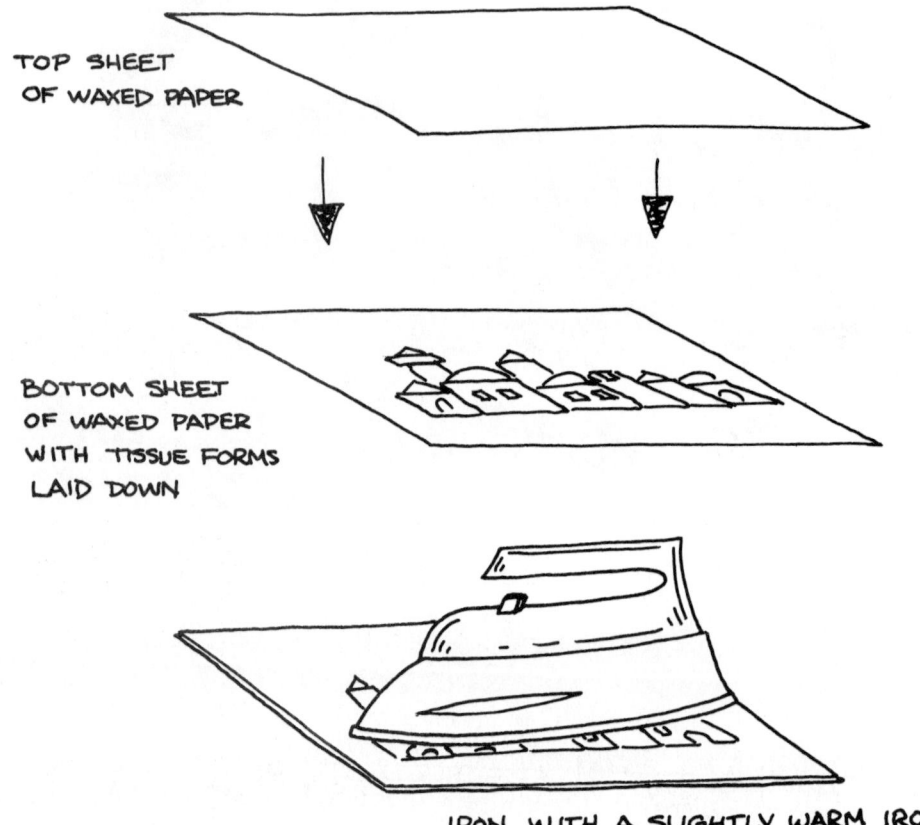

Materials Needed: Waxed paper
precut color tissue paper shapes
warm iron

Allow two sheets of waxed paper per student—about 9"x12" each. Arrange geometric shapes of various colored tissue papers on one piece of the waxed paper to simulate the Jerusalem skyline You may wish to use a small dab of glue or starch to keep the individual pieces of tissue paper in place.

CAREFULLY lay the other piece of waxed paper on top, and iron with a slightly warm iron. The wax will melt and bond the whole into one piece. Since the result is translucent, these make good window decorations. This technique can be adapted to other projects.

EDITOR'S NOTE: If tissue paper is not available, students can draw and color a picture with crayon. When the waxed paper is ironed, the crayon will melt as well, yielding a more modernistic look.

TOP SHEET OF WAXED PAPER

BOTTOM SHEET OF WAXED PAPER WITH TISSUE FORMS LAID DOWN

IRON WITH A SLIGHTLY WARM IRON

Some Simple Help To Make Drawing People Easier

Drawing is the most difficult of the arts because it requires transposing a three-dimensional world into a flat, two-dimensional plane. Since the students live in a 3-D world, using 3-D projects whenever possible is recommended, because they will be more comfortable and have greater success. Nevertheless, there are times when nothing but a drawing will do, and there are ways to make doing it easier. The drawing of the human figure is probably the most difficult task a religious school student is asked to do. Combine that with the intimidation of starting with a blank page, and you have a hurdle accomplished artists dread. Here are three "assists" to help the student over this hurdle and make your life easier.

1. On the blank page, glue half a walnut shell for the head. Now, the student has a point of departure. The task is easier.

2. For humor and movement, invest in some wiggle eyes...the kind found on many stuffed animals. Glue two on the page. Again, the student has a point of departure to start with.

3. For students in second grade and older, an easy way to get proportions is to give each student ten 1 x 2 inch rectangles and a 1-inch diameter circle. Lay out as indicated in the diagram, and students can start moving component parts to introduce movement. Quite a feat for this age level!

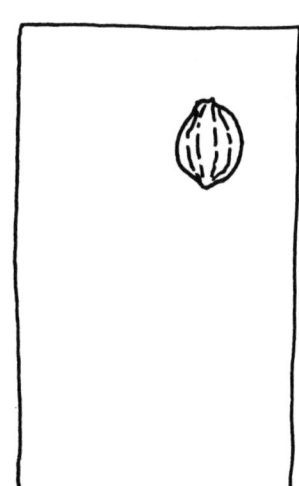

Fast, Clean & Cheap

ORIGAMI (PAPER-FOLDING)

The art of Origami presents one of the least expensive, yet most effective, end products. Origami is the term for the ancient Japanese art of paper folding. Costs are minimal, since newspapers, paper napkins, paper towels, etc., are the only materials. Any library will have books on this subject. The excitement of creating, from commonplace materials, things like a palm tree, a dove of peace, or a flower, never fails to amaze and delight, and makes the learning process exciting.

Origami Project #1— Paper Napkin Flower

Materials needed: 1 lightweight square paper dinner napkin

Fold corners of napkin into center, creasing sharply. Take new corners, and repeat process. Crease sharply. Take new corners and repeat process for a third time. Turn wad over, and turn corners into center again. Crease sharply.

Place triangular side on top of a small inverted glass. Squared side is facing up. Take squared corners, one at a time, and peel downward like an artichoke. Use thumbs to shape petals. Then take the next row of triangular shapes and peel as before. Finally repeat with last row. Invert. The second row of petals will contain the flower. The last row will be mainly decorative. This is a good candy or treat dish for Tu Bish'vat. It is also a good bulletin board decoration.

One side will look like

The other side will look like

Origami Project #2— Star of David

Materials needed: bond, construction or typing paper, 9" x 12"
scissors

This project is a multipurpose Star of David. It can be used for decorative purposes, but can also serve as a tzedakah container, a small gift box, or a letter and envelope combined. Fold as described in the accompanying diagram. If using as a letter and envelope, complete the first four steps before writing the letter so that none of the message appears on the parts that will be cut away.

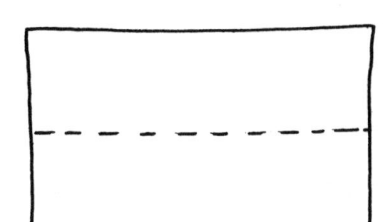

Fig. 1: Fold horizontally and reopen.

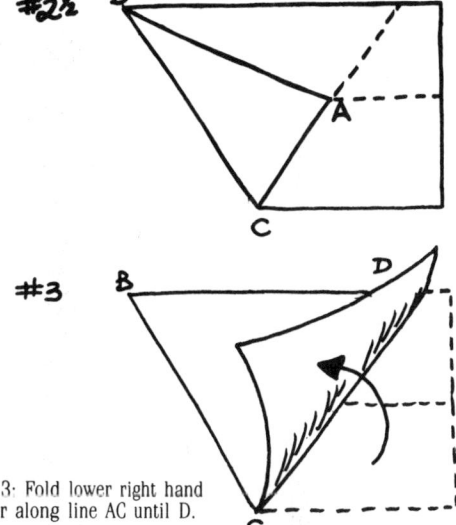

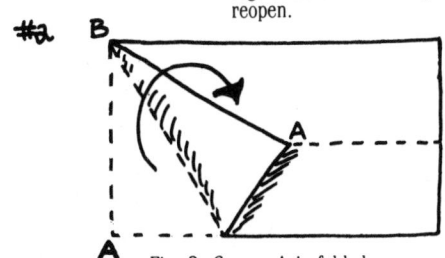

Fig. 2: Corner A is folded over until it touches the horizontal line. Make sure that corner B has a sharp point. Crease line BC.

Fig. 3: Fold lower right hand paper along line AC until D.

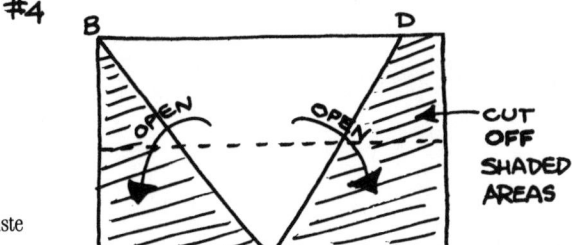

Fig. 4: Open paper. Waste areas on both sides of triangle will be uneven. Cut out triangle. Fold up Point D to E.

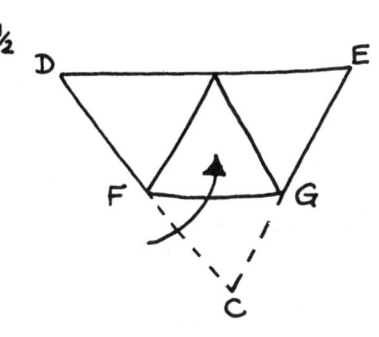

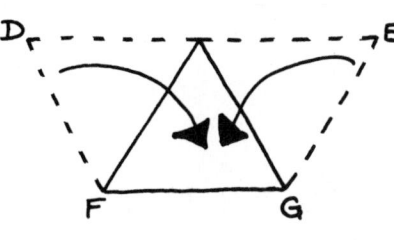

Fig. 5: Fold D to G. Fold E to F. Crease.

Fig. 6: Fold back each point 2/3 of the distance F to G.

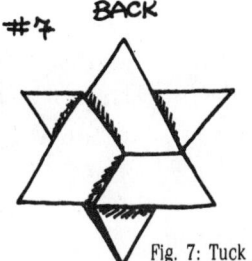

Fig. 7: Tuck back of star points as if closing a carton. This will lock the star.

Fast, Clean & Cheap

Origami Project #3— Hamentashen Candy Dish

Materials needed: 9-inch square of construction paper

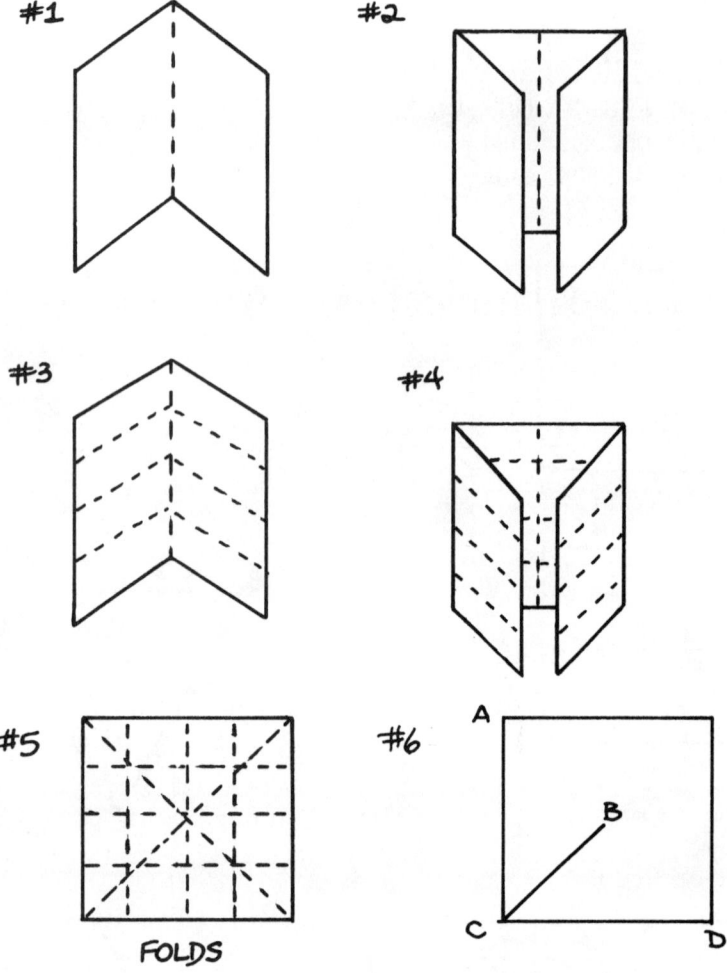

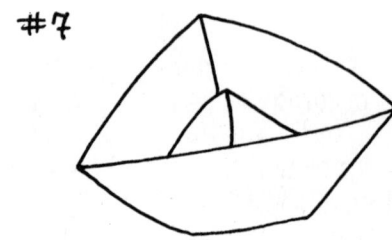

A "hamantash"-shaped candy dish can be made from a 9" square of paper. Fold it in half, open it, and then fold edges in to the center. Turn paper 90 degrees and repeat. Then fold paper diagonally. Reopen. Turn paper over and go through the same procedure. This will weaken the fibers so that the project can be formed more easily. Open paper and make one cut from one corner to the center. Overlap triangle A B C over triangle B C D, gently shaping the paper so that a triangular pyramid is formed in the center. Staple or glue so that the dish is ready for Purim goodies.

COPPER REPOUSSE

Repousse (from the French word meaning "to push out") projects are excellent for middle schoolers and above. The metal imparts a degree of sophistication and permanence. It lends itself to a variety of projects, and will meet the criteria of fast, clean, and cheap! Copper in thin sheets is a metal that is both malleable (bendable, formable) and ductile (able to be stretched and drawn out). It is fairly inexpensive ($1 to $1.50 per square foot, which can yield 4 to 6 projects). Tools are minimal. Two ice cream sticks shaped as shown are the only tools needed. Each person should have a set of these. Some old newspapers plus scissors complete the tool list. Since the copper is very thin, (36 or 40 gauge) it can be cut and divided up with scissors.

The prime idea in repousse is to work with designs that have thickness—not single lines—to give the form.

Use the sharp-pointed ice cream stick to trace or draw the design outline. Always work on several thicknesses of newspaper to cushion the metal. The underlayment of newspaper will provide enough "give" to allow the metal to be stretched. After drawing the outline, turn the copper over. With the metal still on the newspaper, push out (repousse) the areas enclosed within the lines. Reverse again and redraw the outlines to sharpen the image. Reverse, and again push out the areas between the lines from the back. This working from front to back may have to be repeated several times. Copper can be stretched a good 1/4 inch.

NOT USEABLE

General Finishing Instructions

Clean the face of the copper with very fine steel wool (grade 0000), being careful not to dent the raised design. Wipe clean. You can stop here, or, as an option, you can create a rich, antique-looking finish by painting the copper with a weak solution of Liver of Sulphur. It smells like rotten eggs. Rinse thoroughly. Pat very dry. The copper will turn black. Rub with fine steel wool again. The deeply etched details of the design will remain black, giving an antique "tarnished" appearance. When the project is complete, mat or frame it.

IDEAL FORM

Helpful Hints

Tooling copper comes in a variety of gauges or thicknesses. The higher the number, the thinner the metal. A good all-around thickness is 36 gauge.

There is also an aluminum tooling foil. It is much cheaper, but does not stretch as well as the copper, and pierces very easily.

Ice cream stick tools can be recut to keep their sharpness.

The following materials list is the same for all three of the copper repousse projects described below.

Materials needed: thin copper sheets (tooling foil)
newspapers
scissors
corrugated cardboard scraps
ice cream sticks (trimmed to use for shaping)
Liver of Sulphur; small brush (optional)

Fast, Clean & Cheap

Copper Repousse Project #1—Mizraḥ

A mizrah is a wall hanging incorporating Judaic symbols, to be hung on the eastern wall of the home as a reminder of the direction of Jerusalem. An easy way of organizing a design is to arrange the elements of the design at right angles to one another. Items need not be in true scale to other items. Design pattern #1 is a suggestion. The entire design need not be used. Select the elements that are most meaningful to you. In design pattern #2, design elements are overlapped to create NEW decorative forms. This project is basically a repousse picture, and requires only that you follow the basic instructions given above once you have selected your design.

Fast, Clean & Cheap

Copper Repousse Project #2—Mezuzah

Begin by cutting a piece of corrugated cardboard 1" x 3". This is the central shape of the mezuzah form. Design and work the center vertical shape with a design. The letter "SHIN" usually appears on the mezuzah. After working the copper, turn it face down. Place cardboard piece in center. Follow the diagram and neatly fold the piece marked #1 over the cardboard. Then fold over the piece marked #2. It may be easier to do this if you first use the sharp ice cream stick to score the fold lines. Turn mezuzah over. Fold down pieces #3 and #4 neatly to dotted line, and then out. This will create flanges for affixing the mezuzah to the doorpost. The copper, when used outdoors, will develop a lovely green patina.

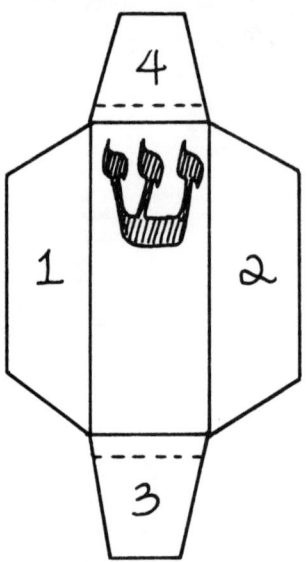
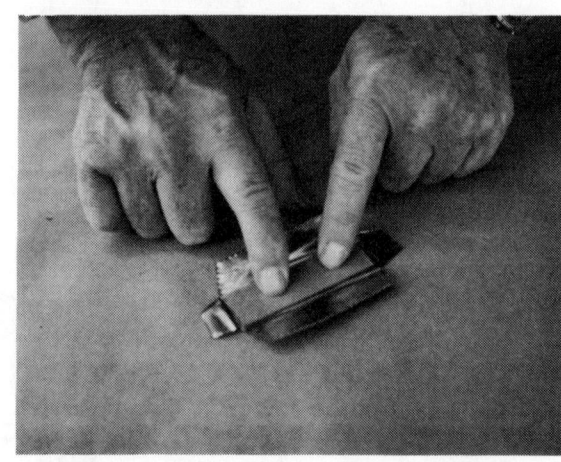
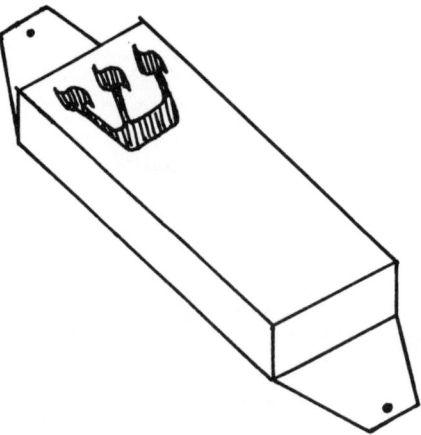

Fast, Clean & Cheap

Copper Repousse
Project #3—Pendant

A copper pendant is a good use of repousse. Cut a 2" square of cardboard. Lay the square on the center of the copper, and draw a trapezoidal flange on each side. Cut out with scissors. Working on newspaper, design and work center section. Then, place finished work face down. Put cardboard square in center. Carefully fold over flange #1, then #2, and then #3. Lay a 25" cord or length of yarn along edge, and fold over flange #4. The copper is rigid enough to hold the cord in place. Knot to proper length.

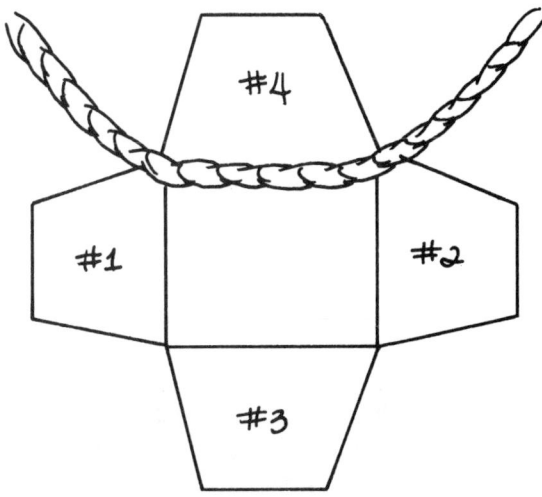

Fast, Clean & Cheap

CLAY PROJECTS

Generally, water-base clays are not recommended for the religious school because of the mess and lack of firing facilities. This type of clay, dried and unfired, is very fragile. Most items would be broken before they arrived home. Here are two clay projects utilizing oil clay (Plasticene, Permoplast, plastic modeling clay, etc.) These oil-base clays never dry out and can be used and reused. Save all crumbs. Oil clay is more expensive than water clay, and is sold in 1- or 2-pound blocks.

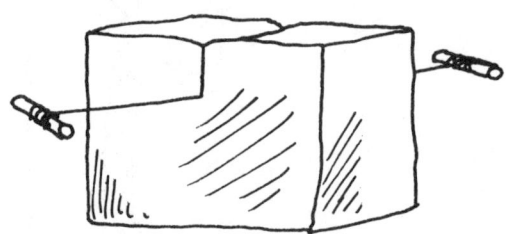

A thin wire wrapped around two dowels or pencils makes a good wire cutter for easy slicing of the clay. Knives drag through the clay and make a strenuous mess. (This way, pretend you are cutting halvah!)

Use tagboard or index cards as a base when using oil clay—their slick surface will prevent much oil absorption and allow a much longer working time. In addition to the types of projects described below, of course, clay is the most basic of sculpting materials. Oil-based clay can be used over and over to create three-dimensional figures to illustrate Bible stories or historical events, make relief maps, or serve as a base for landscape scenes in dioramas or model kibbutzim.

Clay Project #1— Tablets of the Law

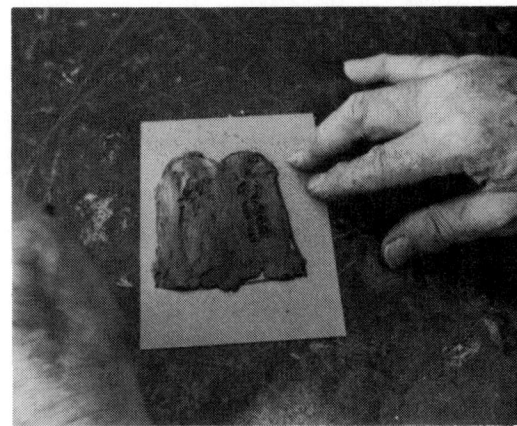

Materials needed: index cards, 4" x 6"
clay
toothpicks, nails or other tools to add detail

Have each student spread a thin layer of clay on a 4" x 6" index card. Each student should be given an amount equal to 1 to 2 pats of butter. Using a stylus, nail or toothpick, students can then draw the two Tablets of the Law and the appropriate letters. Any mistakes can easily be smudged over, and redrawn.

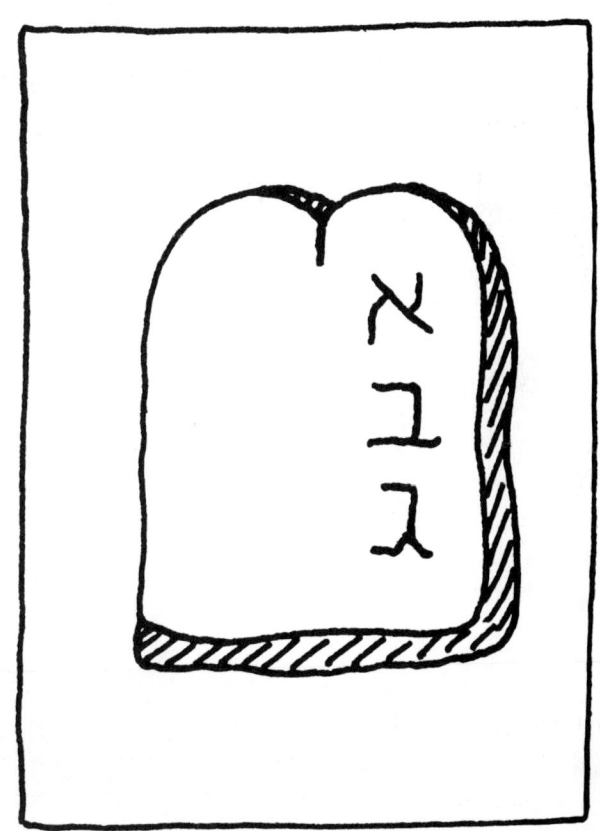

Fast, Clean & Cheap

Clay Project #2— Western Wall

Materials needed: same as for Clay Project #1

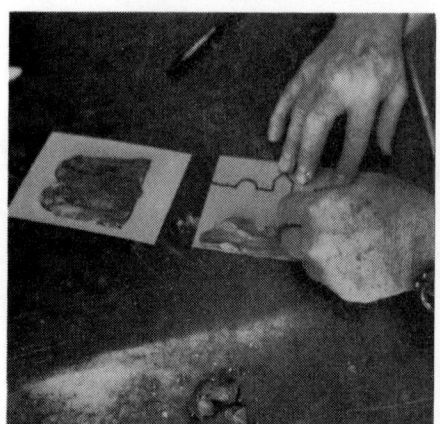

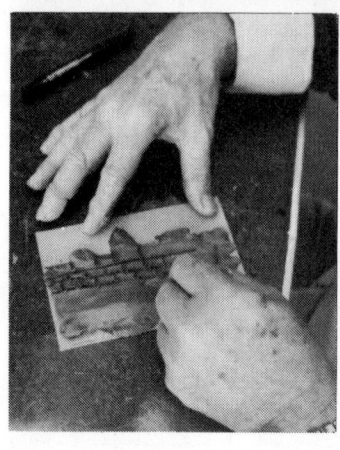

On a 4" x 6" plain white index card, the teacher can draw a simple crenellated line, possibly with a tower or two. This represents the Jerusalem skyline at the Western Wall. Using a pat of oil clay about the size of 2 butter pats, students should spread the clay with the fingers to cover the area beneath the line. With a stylus or toothpick, the student can draw in the rock patterns of the wall. Any errors can be smudged over with the fingers and redrawn. The oil in the clay does make a bit of a bond with the index card, and these are effective on bulletin boards.

BINGO GAMES

Students love playing BINGO games. These can be tremendous learning experiences in the guise of entertainment. The games can be adapted to a variety of learning experiences. Here are examples, from one for beginners to one for teenagers. While the making of BINGO cards isn't strictly "art," it does allow for some individual expression and provides a visual learning aid.

Bingo Game #1— Aleph-Bet Bingo

Materials needed: plain paper or photocopies of 9-square card
pencils, markers or crayons
heavy paper, index cards or game discs
scissors

For the beginner, a nine square card is a good start. The teacher can provide photocopies of the card from this book, or students can make their own. Any piece of paper can be divided into nine equal squares or rectangles by folding it in thirds, unfolding, and then folding in thirds in the opposite direction. Have all students write the letter "aleph" in the center. Then let each student add eight more letters, assuming they have learned at least nine. Students may place the letters in any order. This will make it unlikely that two cards will be alike. Teacher calls letters, one by one. Winner has three in a row horizontally, vertically or diagonally. Variations might be covering all four corners or five squares in an "X" shape. Tailor the game to your students' grade level, capability and attention span. To insure that numbers are called randomly, cut heavy paper or index cards into small squares, and write one letter on each. Then draw the letters from a box. Similar blank squares of paper or card stock can be used to mark cards if you don't have BINGO markers and want to use the cards more than one time.

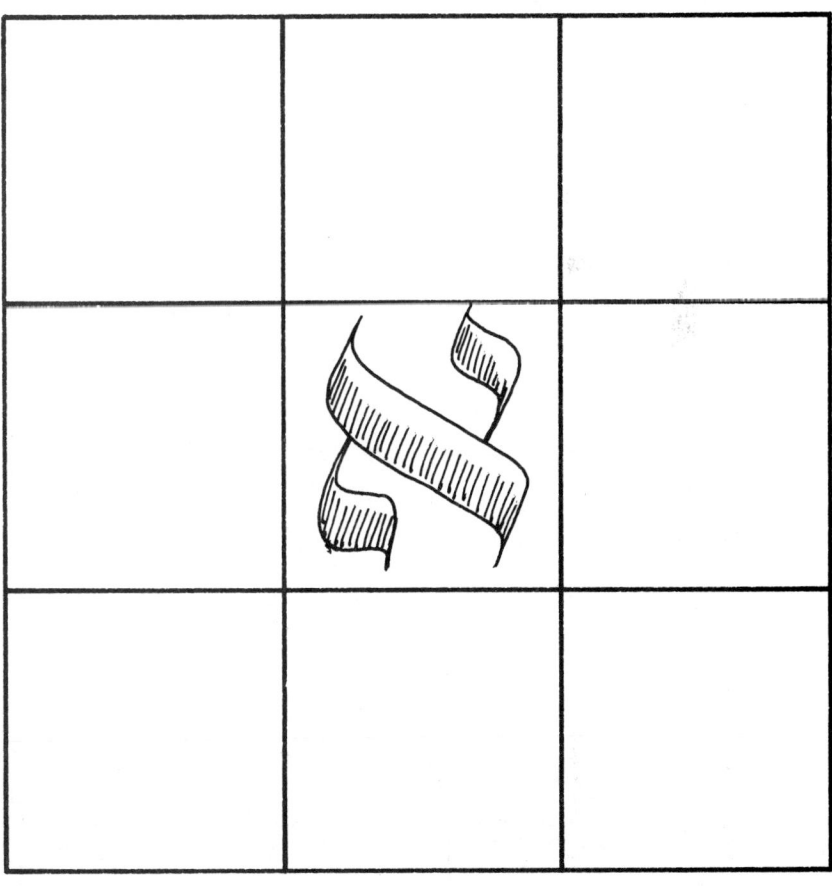

Fast, Clean & Cheap

Bingo Game #2— Twelve Tribes Bingo

Materials needed: photocopies of BINGO card on the following page
materials listed in BINGO Game #1

For more advanced students, this is an example of a way to make a game primarily a learning experience. Start by giving each student a photocopy of the Twelve Tribes BINGO board from this book. Students place the names of the listed tribes in any order on the Bingo board, in the blank spaces. Then the teacher calls off spaces at random. A foolproof method to insure that there is no chance of favoritism is to have the teacher fill out a card, cut up the squares and place them in a hat from which they are drawn. Winners must cover five spaces in a row horizontally, vertically, diagonally. As in BINGO Game #1 above, variations can also be used; just be sure to lay out the ground rules beforehand.

Remember, this is a learning experience, with the game as a highlight and a visual reinforcement. After the BINGO boards are ready, discuss the tribes in general—how they came to be, heritage, lineage, historical setting, etc. Continue by talking a bit about each of the individual tribes —

What was the symbol for each?

What was the occupation of each?

Who was the oldest?

Who was the youngest?—and so on.

Then, begin the game, but when calling a tribe's name or symbol, describe it with a question. Some examples:

Whose land share was divided between his sons, Ephraim and Manesseh? (Joseph)

What must be kosher, but is never eaten? (Torah scrolls)

Who was swift as a deer? (Naphtali)

What symbol appears on a mezuzah? (the letter Shin)

What symbol stands for life? (Ḥai)

And so on. These questions can be tailored to the level of the students. They can also be a springboard for further discussions.

1. Reuben
2. Simeon
3. Levi
4. Judah
5. Zebulun
6. Issachar
7. Dan
8. Gad
9. Asher
10. Naphtali
11. Benjamin
12. Joseph

Fast, Clean & Cheap

Follow the Dots

Students love follow-the-dot games. For the beginner, here is an "aleph" laid out with numbered dots. Have student start at number 1 and follow in sequence, using straight lines.

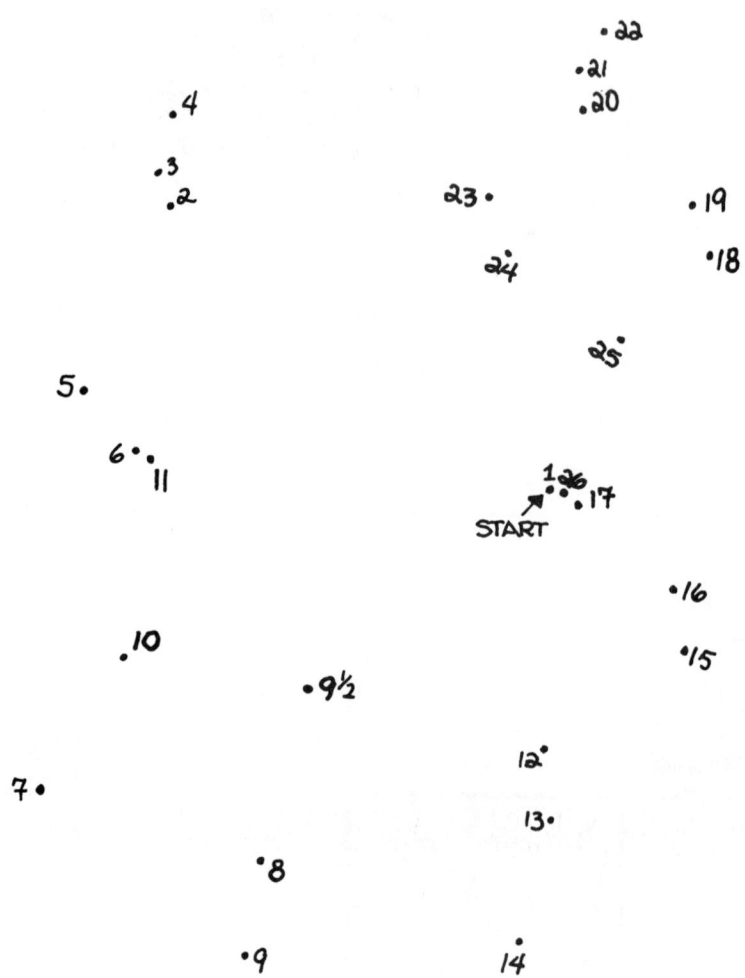

I've also included some other ready-made follow-the-dot puzzles on the following page, but the real reason for including this section is that these are teaching games that anyone can make to use with any subject matter—any letter, simple design, or symbol. To make the puzzle, use any already printed material as your base. Overlay design or letter with onion-skin paper, tracing paper, or acetate. Place dots on the overlay at strategic points along the lines of the design, remembering that connecting lines will be straight. Number the dots on the overlay CONSECUTIVELY. Then photocopy or duplicate overlay.

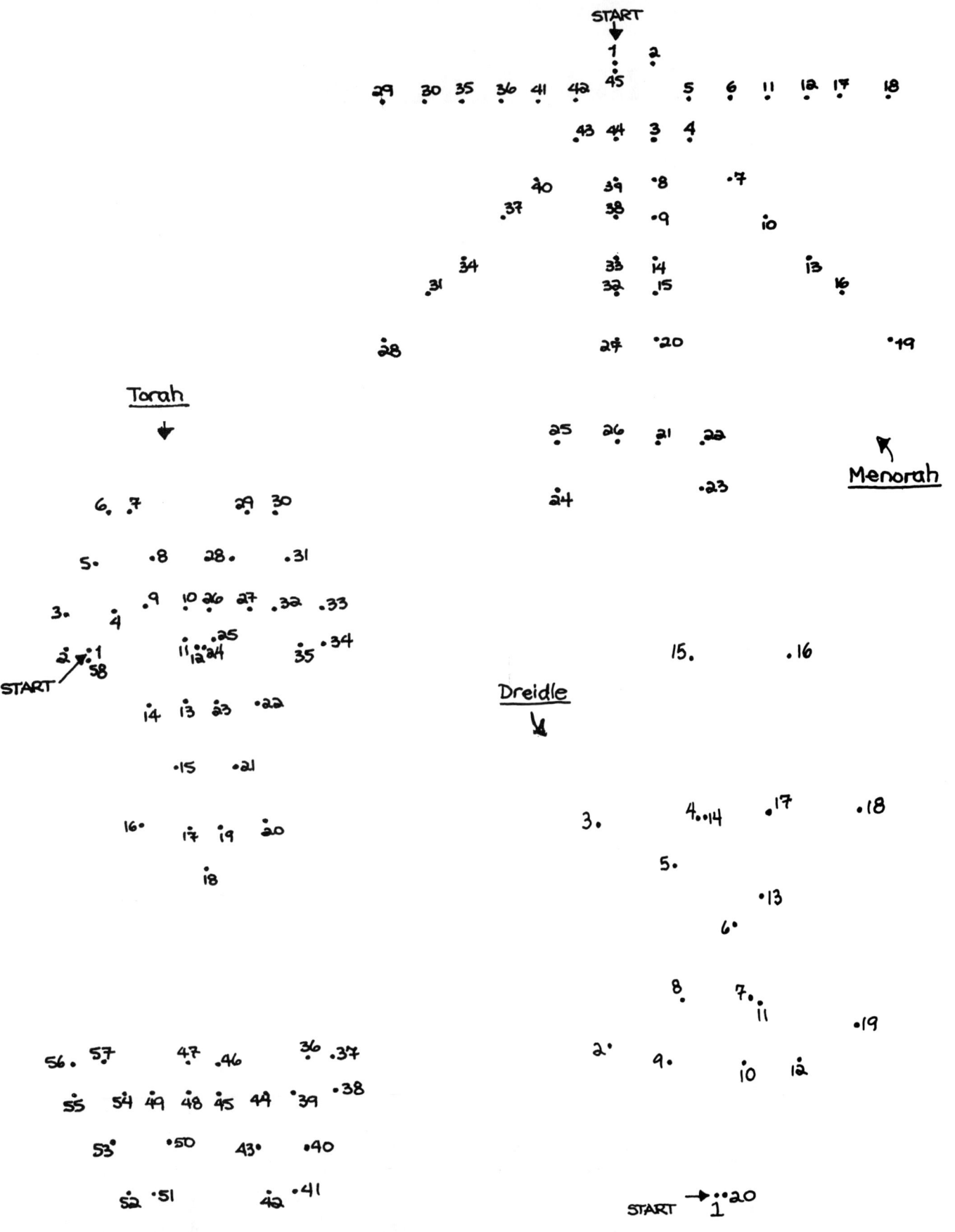

FOR MORE ADVANCED STUDENTS, THE NUMBERING CAN BE DONE IN HEBREW.

Fast, Clean & Cheap

Edible Judaism

Here is another very simple idea that can be used for many different purposes. For each student, spread a slice of challah or bread with a smooth layer of softened cream cheese or peanut butter. Then give each student a handful of raisins to create a Judaic design, symbol or letter. Even short Hebrew words and names can be spelled out this way. This is a double-barrelled learning exercise—the information is processed through four of the five senses (sight, smell, taste and touch) as well as intellectually.

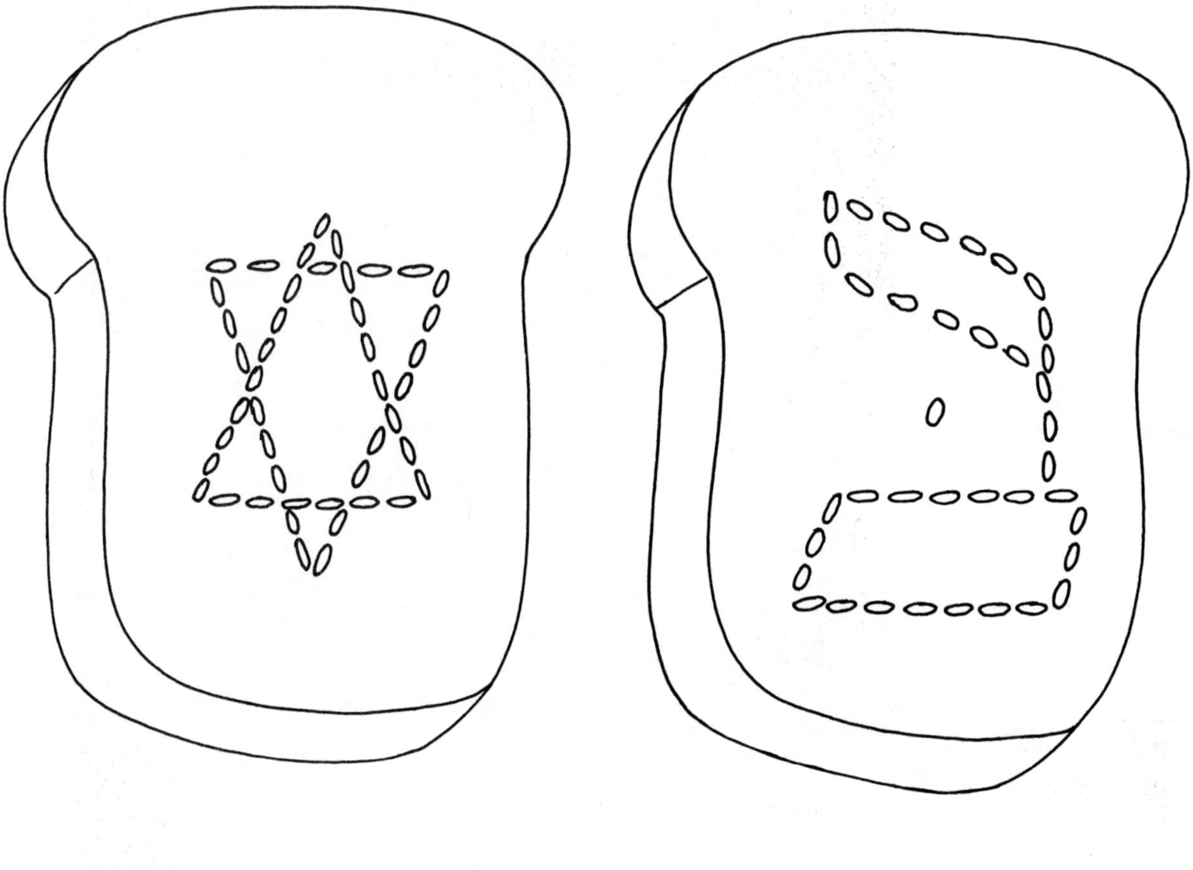

OTHER IDEAS:

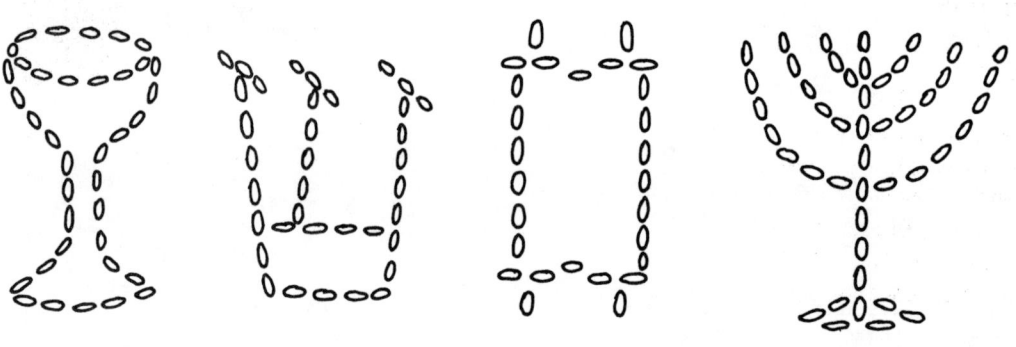

46

Fast, Clean & Cheap

SOME WAYS TO ADD PEP TO "PLAIN OLD PICTURES"

I mentioned earlier that today's students are exposed to sophisticated visual effects constantly, so that it's difficult to convince them that they can actually make an effective picture themselves. "Just plain drawing" seems dull and difficult to many students. The ideas that follow are ways to make a simple shape or picture seem more impressive without the mess that attends painting. All of them can be adapted to various uses, including greeting cards, illustrations, wall or bulletin board decorations, placemats, book covers, etc. Several of the examples use the simple shape of the Magen David, but any other simple shape can be used, and some of the ideas can even be used for fairly complex drawings.

Fast, Clean & Cheap

Design Idea #1— A Pull Apart Picture

Materials needed: two pieces of construction paper in contrasting colors
scissors
paste

Cut a Magen David (or other shape) from construction paper. Then cut it apart into many pieces like a puzzle. Arrange them in order as you cut them apart. Arrange the pieces on a sheet of contrasting colored paper with even spaces in between cut pieces. Paste down. This would also be effective if used with a picture drawn by a student as long as the elements of the picture had strong outlines.

Fast, Clean & Cheap

Design Idea #2—Magical Mystical Chalk Picture

Materials needed: white paper
pencil
white (casein) glue
colored chalk

Draw a design on white paper with pencil. Squeeze white glue evenly but thickly on pencil lines. Dry very thoroughly. Then, horizontally smudge different colors of chalk with the finger or cotton swabs. The slickness of the dried glue will prevent the chalk from adhering. The result will be a magical, mystical chalk picture.

Fast, Clean & Cheap

Design Idea #3— Starburst Designs

Materials needed: cut-out Magen David or other shape
white paper
crayons

A tagboard Star of David (or other shape) is placed in the center of a sheet of paper. Student holds down the cut-out shape with one hand and makes a series of radiating crayon lines from the center of the shape, extending the lines out onto the clean paper, with the other hand. When the pattern is lifted, a negative image of the star (or other shape) will appear. This is a good reinforcement project for students with weaker drawing skills. Multi-colored crayons will add to the excitement.

Design Idea #4— Contrast Designs

Materials needed: 1 sheet white paper 12" x 18"
1 sheet black paper 9" x 12"
scissors
paste

This easy positive-negative contrast design technique creates a striking finished product. Using plant forms, these make dramatic designs for Sukkot or Shavuot, but many other designs can be used just as effectively.

Begin by cutting the black paper into three 3" x 12" strips. On one edge of one black paper strip, draw and then cut 1/2 of a leaf, flower or other symmetrical form. Paste negative area at right edge of white paper. Flip over cut out black paper form and paste on white paper to complete the design.

Repeat with two other strips, using the same or different flowers, leaves or designs. This will result in a very dramatic decorative panel.

Fast, Clean & Cheap

Paper Chain Wall Decorations

This very simple project will result in EVERY student's being represented in a room wall decoration. While the specific instructions below apply this technique in the form of a hanukkiah, any simple shape can be used.

Materials needed: paper strips, appx. 1/2" x 5"
paste (unless paper strips are gummed)
stapler

Make paper chain. Either precut, gummed paper strips or homemade paper strips may be used—even combined. Start by making one loop—then interlock each succeeding loop, using library paste to join ends of paper strips.

Students will work at different speeds and levels of dexterity. It doesn't make any difference. The total effect will be greater than the sum of the parts.

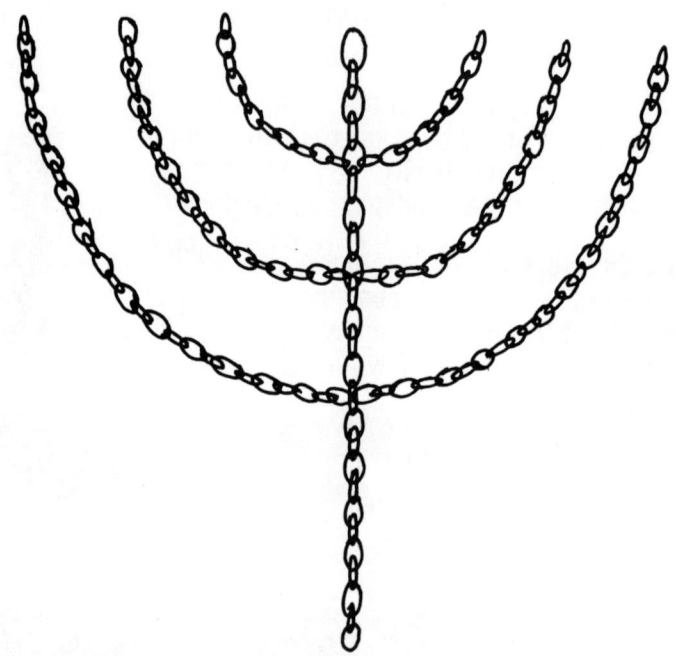

When a total of about 25 feet of chain is made, start to assemble on the bulletin board using a stapler. Center menorah post can be about 30 inches high. Menorah arms need not be of continuous pieces. Short lengths can be stapled to the bulletin board without any loss of effect.

MORE CLASSROOM PROJECTS

The advantage of knowledge and skill in particular artistic techniques, like some of those described in the last section, is that they can be applied to many different subject matters and can yield many variations. The disadvantage of this approach, however, is that the person who has to come up with the ideas for new variations (and make the patterns, and write the instructions, and make test samples) is YOU, the teacher. While I encourage you to do this if you have the interest, ability, and time, I've also collected (and invented) a wide selection of "one-shot" projects—specific ideas for producing specific objects. Complete instructions and detailed diagrams mean that these projects are ready to go—you need only to gather the materials. Best of all, every one of them meets our criteria: they are **FAST, CHEAP** and **CLEAN!**

Paper Kippah (Yarmulke)

Materials needed: one sheet construction paper, 9" x 12"
scissors
stapler
materials for decorating if desired

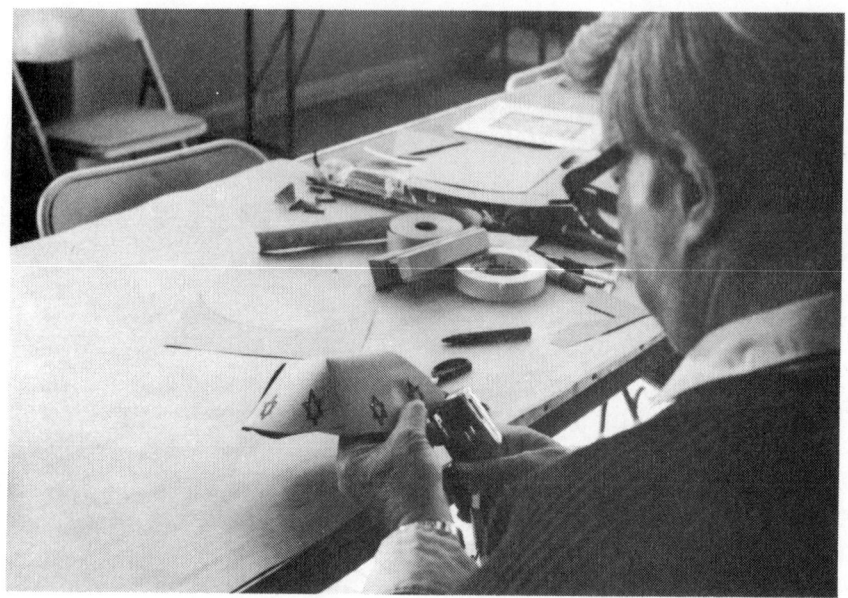

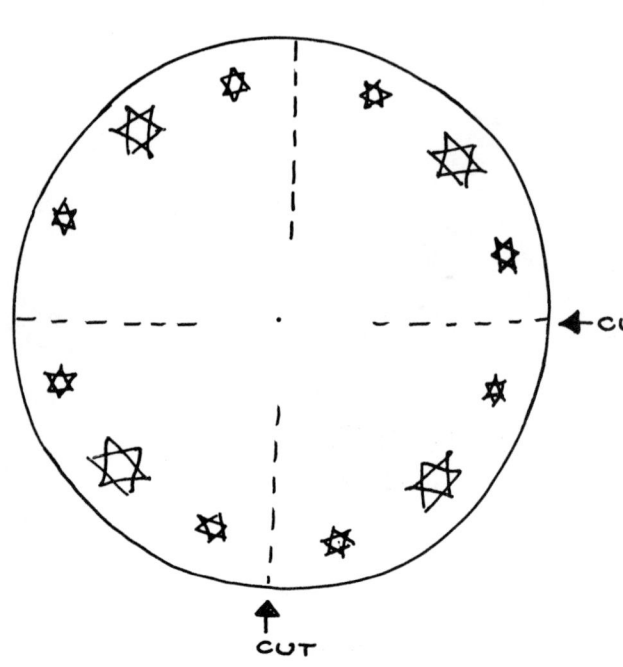

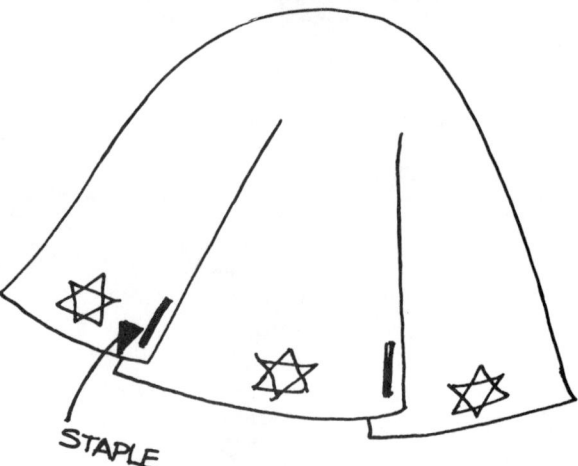

From the sheet of construction paper, which may be any color, cut a 9-inch circle. Then make four straight cuts from the edge of the circle to about 1-1/2 inches from center, as in the diagram. If the kippah is to be decorated, the decoration should be added at this point, before shaping the kippah. Then, overlap the cut edges about one inch to shape the kippah and staple. The larger the overlap, the smaller the kippah.

Three Dimensional Paper Animals

Materials needed: 9" x 12" construction paper, various colors
scissors
stapler
crayons or markers (to add details)

Animals figure prominently in a number of biblical episodes, and children are often ask to draw animals to illustrate these stories. If an animal can be made three-dimensional, it will have greater impact and reality. An easy pattern is made by folding and cutting a 9 x 12 inch sheet of paper as shown below.

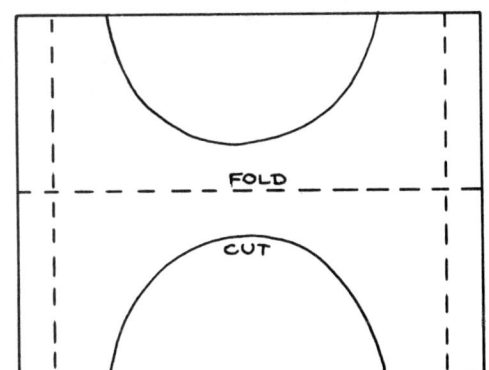

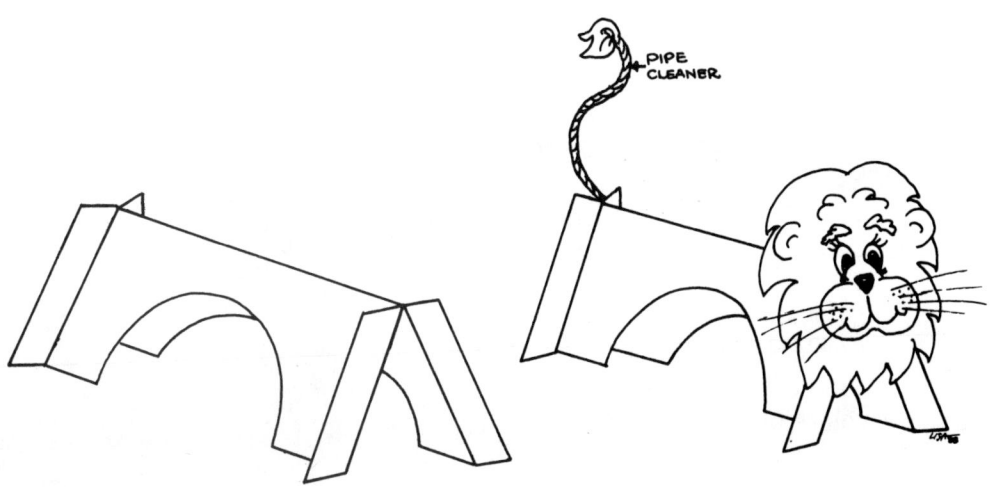

Fold on dotted lines—cut on solid lines. This is the body foundation. Add heads, tails, details, etc. For tall animals (e.g., giraffes) fold paper in other direction.

Fast, Clean & Cheap

Double Name Contour Drawing (Hebrew)

Materials needed: drawing paper, 9" x 12" or larger
crayons or markers
black crayon

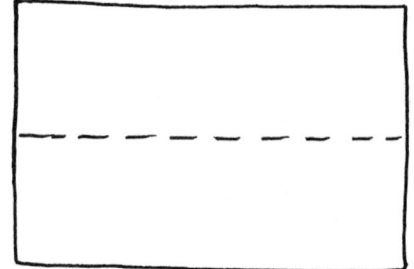

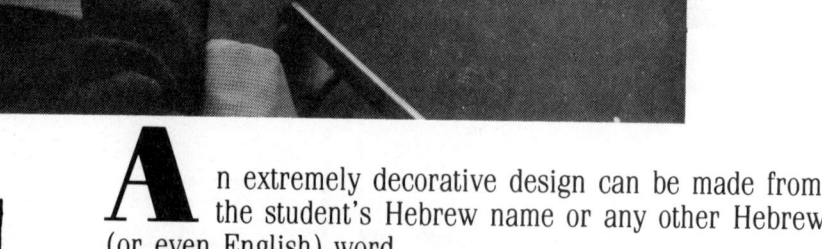

An extremely decorative design can be made from the student's Hebrew name or any other Hebrew (or even English) word.

Fold the piece of drawing paper in half the long way and crease.

Then, open the paper and write the Hebrew name (or other word) on the creased line with black crayon. Fold up again and press and rub. This will transfer a mirror image of the name onto the adjacent half of the paper. Draw around names with a colored marker or crayon. Draw succeeding lines larger and with other colors of crayons and/or markers.

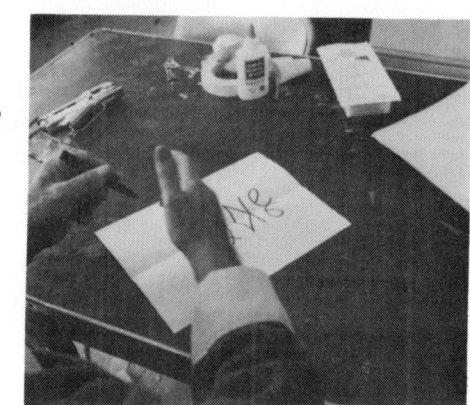

Fast, Clean & Cheap

Multi Design Hebrew Name

Materials needed: drawing paper, 9" x 12"
crayons or markers

Divide the paper into 32 equal rectangles (1 1/2" x 2"), either by folding or with a ruler. Starting in the box at the upper right corner, write your name in Hebrew over and over again, one letter to a space. Fill in the entire page, going as far as you can. Treat each boxed letter as a different design.

Fast, Clean & Cheap

Judaic Wind Sock

Materials needed: construction paper, 9″ x 12″ (blue or white)
narrow 12-inch strips of paper in white and shades of blue
tissue or crepe paper (blue and white)
scissors, stapler, paste

On a 9″ x 12″ sheet of paper (white or blue) paste several 12-inch paper strips of white and other shades of blue. Along one 12-inch edge of the colored paper, paste 1″ x 20″-inch strips of blue and white tissue paper or crepe paper streamers.

Form 9″ x 12″ paper into a cylinder. Paste or staple together. Add a paper strip for a handle or a hanger.

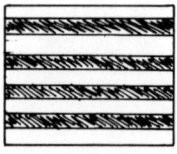

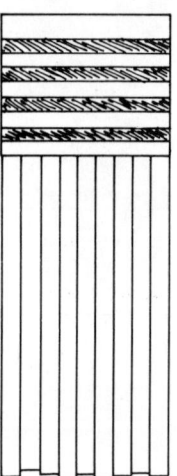

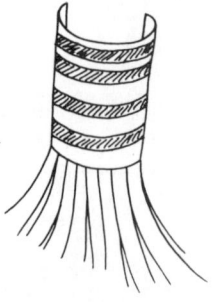

Seder Plate

Materials needed: 9" plain white paper plate
10" square of clear Contact paper
scissors
crayons

Draw symbols of the Passover foods around the plate with crayons and/or markers. Add religious symbols. When done, cover the plate with the square of clear contact paper (a square slightly larger than the plate will compensate for the plate's curve). Trim corners. Now you have an inexpensive Passover plate that can safely be used with food—and wiped clean after use.

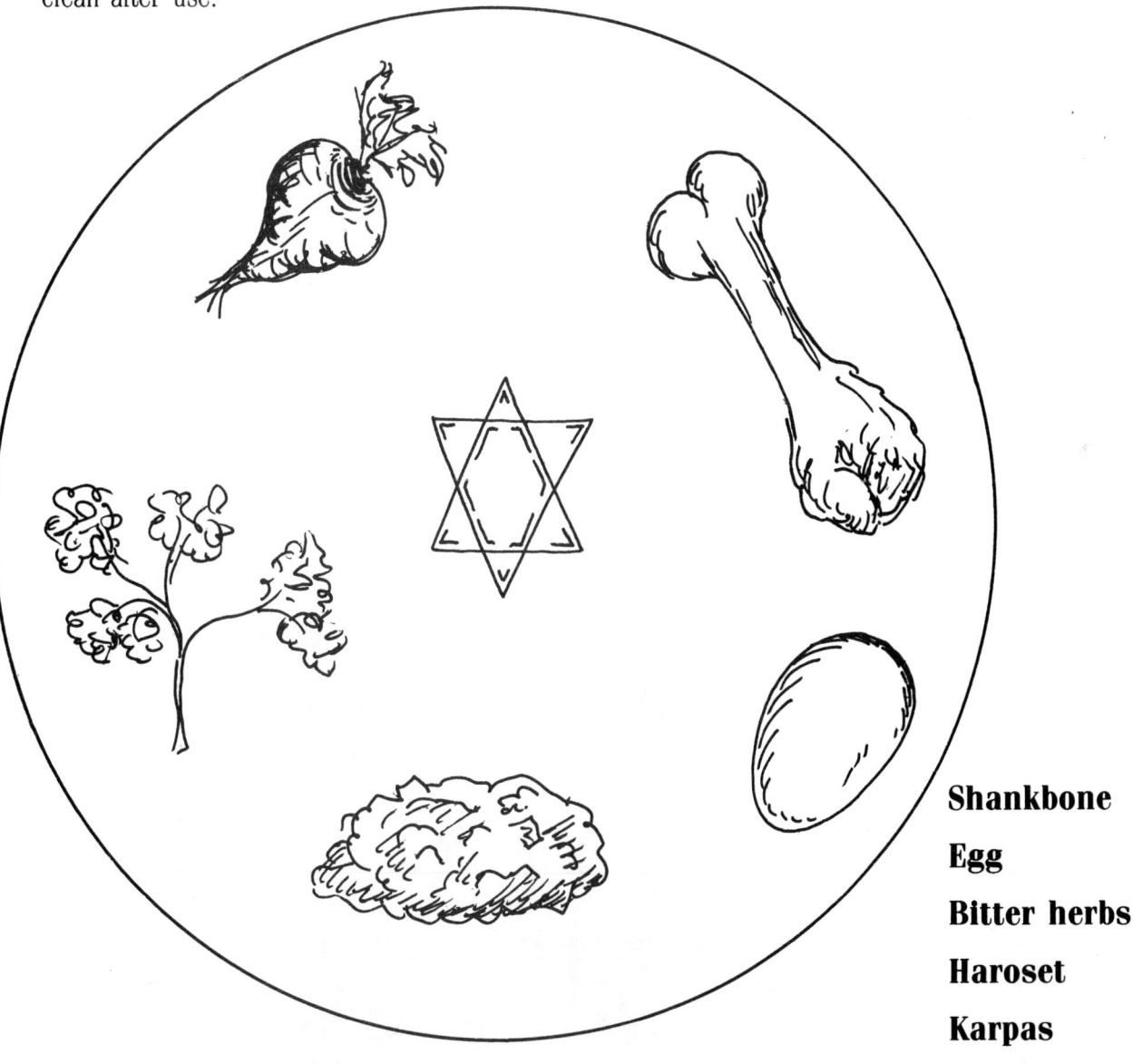

Shankbone

Egg

Bitter herbs

Haroset

Karpas

Fast, Clean & Cheap

Matzah Cover

Materials needed: 2 pieces bleached or unbleached muslin, 12" x 18"
needle and thread or sewing machine
fabric crayons, ribbon, etc. (for decoration)

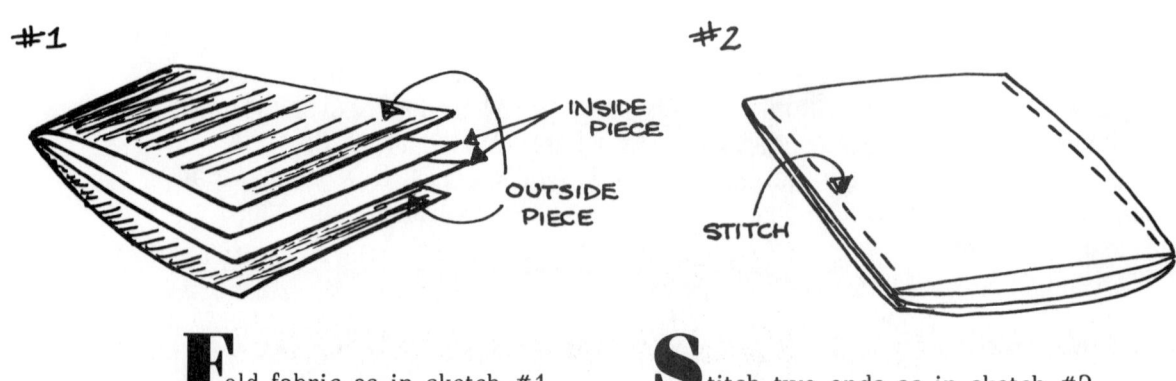

Fold fabric as in sketch #1.

Stitch two ends as in sketch #2.

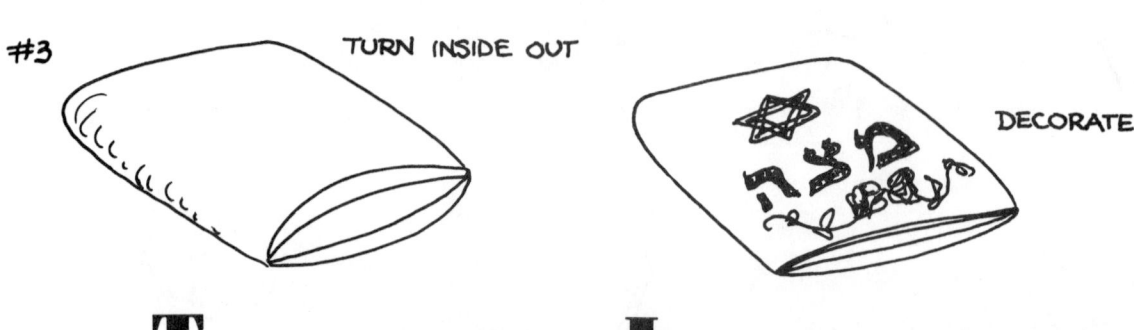

Turn one pocket inside out.

Iron, and then decorate as desired.

This will produce a matzah cover that has the three necessary pockets, and which is inexpensive and quick to make.

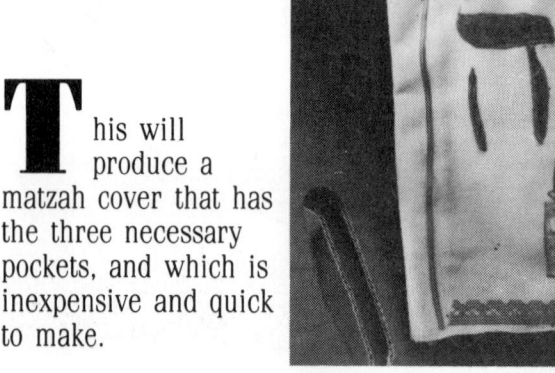

Fast, Clean & Cheap

Kiddush Cup (Elijah's Cup)

Materials needed: three 3-oz. paper cups
a 9-inch square of aluminum foil
masking tape

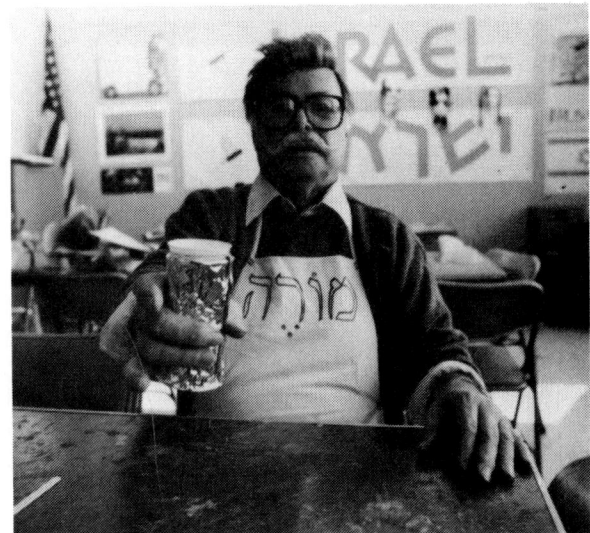

A usable, drinkable kiddush cup can easily and cheaply be made.

Tape 2 cups together as in illustration (with bottoms together).

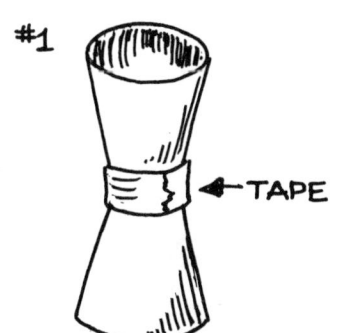

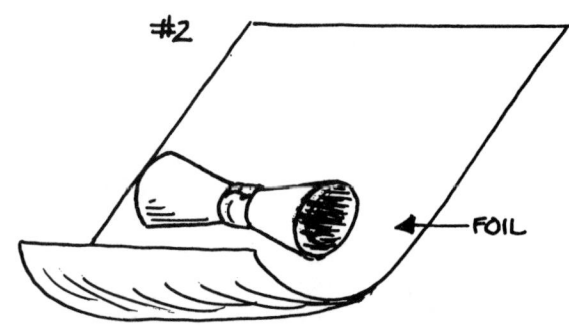

Roll up the two taped cups in the aluminum foil. Tuck ends of foil into the open ends of cups. Gently, squeeze foil around cups. Be careful not to crush cups.

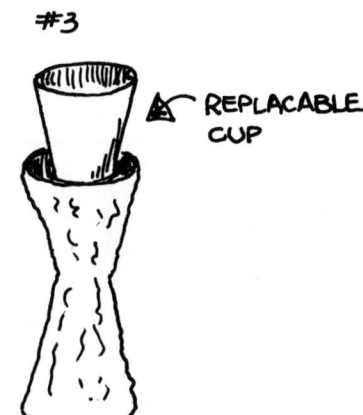

Place third cup into opening at top. This can be drunk from and replaced easily when soiled. L'Hayyim!

Fast, Clean & Cheap

Drinking Straw Dreidel

Materials needed: 4 drinking straws
construction paper
scissors
masking tape

Cut straws down to about 6-8 inches, making sure that they are all equal in length. With masking tape, tape all four straws together at both ends. Straw ends will form a square (see illustration).

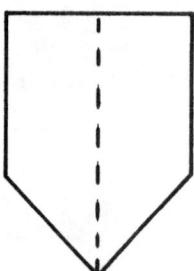 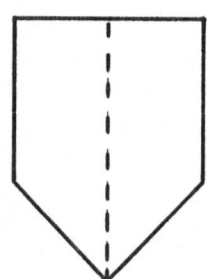

Cut 2 pieces of construction paper as shown in the illustration. Fold each piece in half.

Insert pieces so that the "fins" are separated by the straws. (See cross section.)

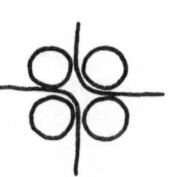

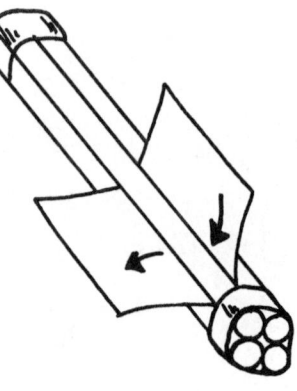

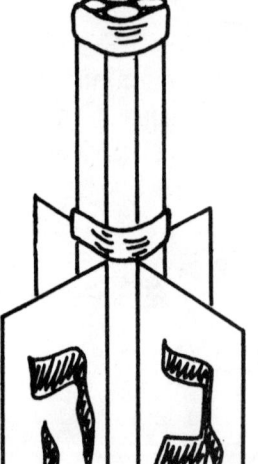

Place a ring of tape around the straws just above the top of the "fins" to secure them in place. Decorate with appropriate letters and symbols.

Pin the Shammash on the Ḥanukkiah

Materials needed: wrapping or butcher paper about 18" x 36"
drawing materials or colored paper (to make Hanukkiah picture)
masking tape
scraps of heavy red, orange and/or yellow paper

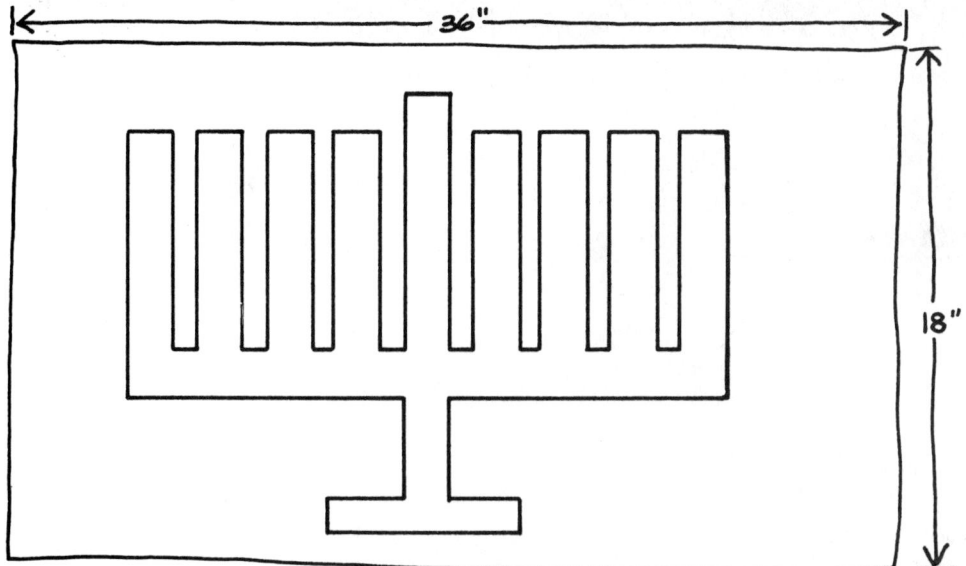

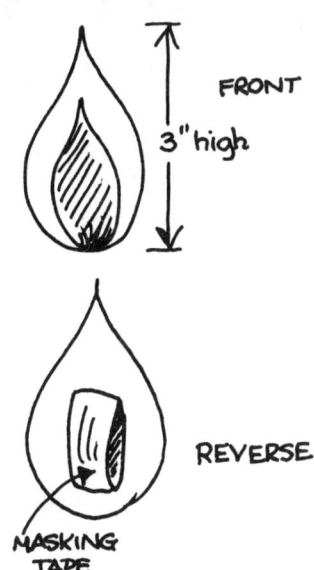

This is a variation on the old "Pin the Tail on the Donkey" game. On a large piece of butcher or wrapping paper, draw a large Hanukkiah. This can also be done by gluing or pasting strips of colored paper. It pays to make a good Hanukkiah —it can be used year after year. Mount the paper so that the center of the paper is at about eye level of the average student. Generally, this would be mounted on a chalkboard or wall which will not accommodate pins or tacks. (They are dangerous for younger children.)

Make a flame of orange, red, and/or yellow paper. Markers and crayons can also be used. Students might want to make their own. Place each student's name at the bottom of the flame for identification. Make a loop out of masking tape (about 4 inches long) with the gummed side out. Place on back of each student's flame. With the appropriate hoop-la, blindfold students, one at a time. Give them their flames, turn them 8 times (one for each day of Hanukkah), and let them affix their flames. The one nearest to the shammash wins.

STAR OF DAVID

The Star or Shield of David—the Magen David—is the most commonly used and most widely recognized symbol of Judaism, at least in North America. Thus, you'll find it handy to have many variations of it to use in decorations and to adorn other projects. A few appear below, and others can be found in the "Design Ideas" and "Origami" sections of the chapter that describes general art and craft techniques.

1) Magic Triangle

Materials needed: precut equilateral triangles
                             pencils (or crayons) and paper for tracing

The geometric concept of the Star of David is extremely complex for primary students to comprehend. A simple way to help them draw and understand is to use equilateral triangles, about 2-3 inches on a side. Give each student two of the triangles and let them experiment with the placement of one over the other until the Magen David is achieved. Then trace the outline. Students a bit older can be given one triangle to trace, with the flat side on the bottom. After tracing, they can pick up the triangle and reposition it so that the point is on the bottom, and then trace again. *Voila—a Jewish star!*

2) Drinking Straw (Linear) Star

Materials needed: 6 thin paper drinking straws
pipe cleaners
scissors
glue

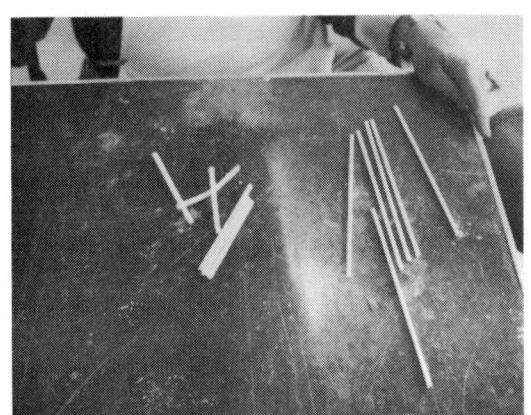

Cut pipe cleaners into 4-inch lengths. Then, take 6 drinking straws of equal length and 6 of the 4-inch pieces of pipe cleaners. Create two triangles by inserting bent pipe cleaners into straw ends to connect them. Lay one triangle on top of the other to create a star. Small drops of glue at points of contact will give you a good decorative star. Paint, sequins and glitter may also be added. If straws are waxed or made of plastic, they may be hard to paint. A few drops of liquid soap in the paint usually solves the problem. Stars of different sizes can be made by cutting straws into various lengths, but be sure that all six pieces to be used in making one star are the same length (unless you specifically want to create assymetrical stars).

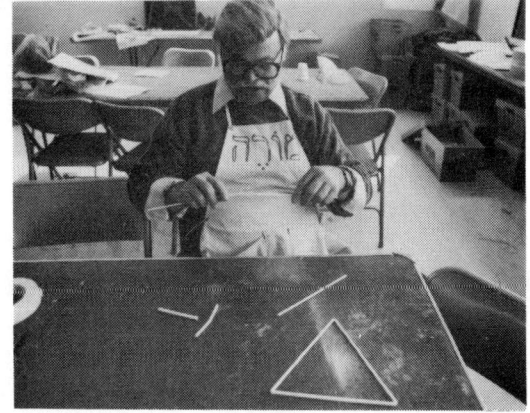

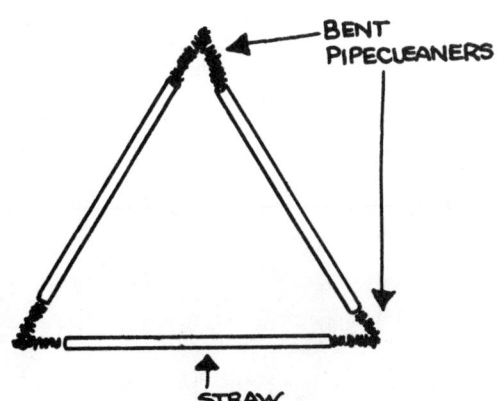

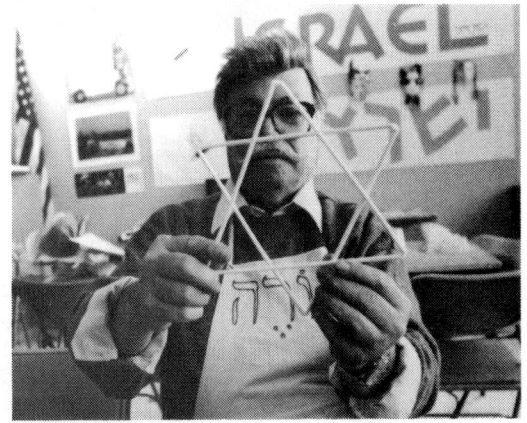

Fast, Clean & Cheap

3) A One-Cut Star of David

Materials needed: 9" square of paper
scissors

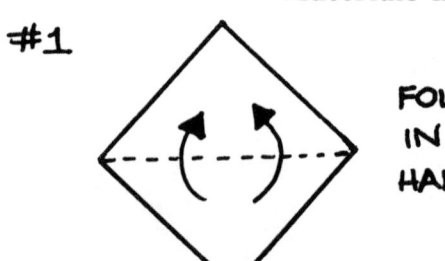

#1 FOLD IN HALF

Fold a nine-inch square of paper in half on dotted line.

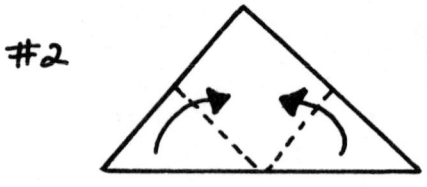

#2 FOLD UP ENDS IN THIRDS

From center point on fold, fold up ends in thirds. Each fold should be made at a 60-degree angle.

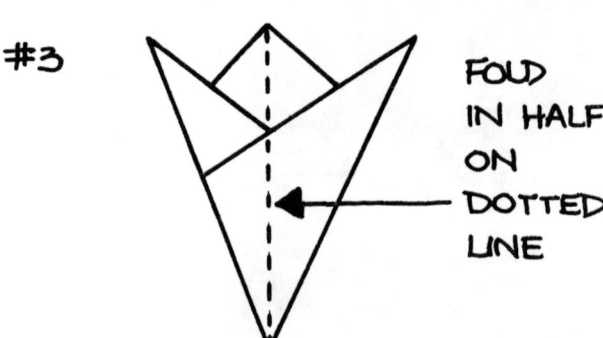

#3 FOLD IN HALF ON DOTTED LINE

Fold in half on dotted line.

Cut on dotted line.

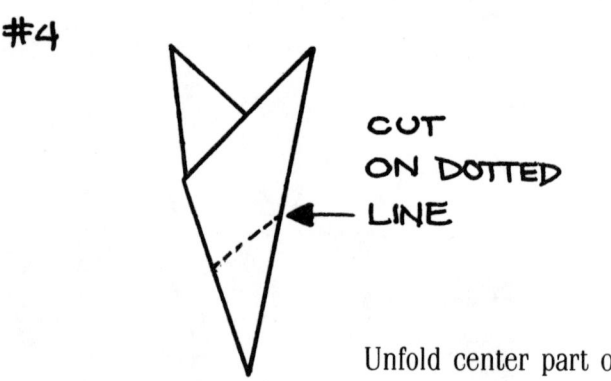

#4 CUT ON DOTTED LINE

Unfold center part of paper.

LO! A ONE-CUT STAR OF DAVID!

#5 UNFOLD CENTER PART OF PAPER

66 Fast, Clean & Cheap

4) Magen David Pinwheel

Materials needed: 9" square of paper
paper scraps in a contrasting color
marker or crayon same color as scraps
a new pencil with an eraser
tiny glass beads
scissors
straight pin or T-pin

For each pinwheel, use a 9-inch square of paper. Cut from the corners diagonally to within one inch of the center.

Gently, pull points marked with dots in the illustration to the center WITHOUT creasing, and use a large straight pin or a T-pin to secure shaped pinwheel into a pencil eraser. A glass bead on each side of the pinwheel will enable it to turn easily.

Color in the triangle at each corner, as indicated. Paste a triangle of the same size and color over the colored triangle to complete the Magen David Pinwheel.

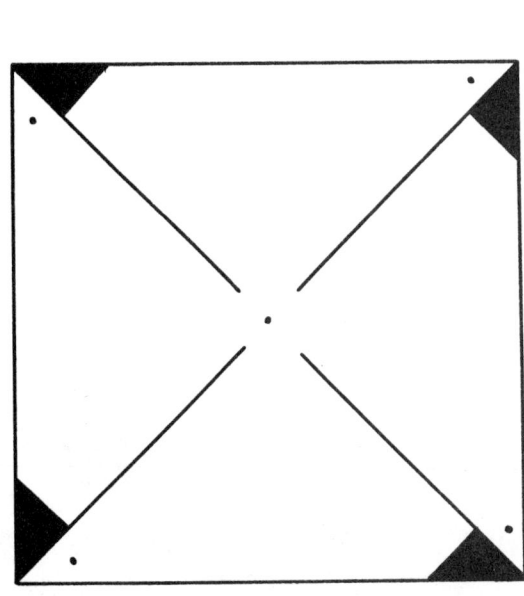
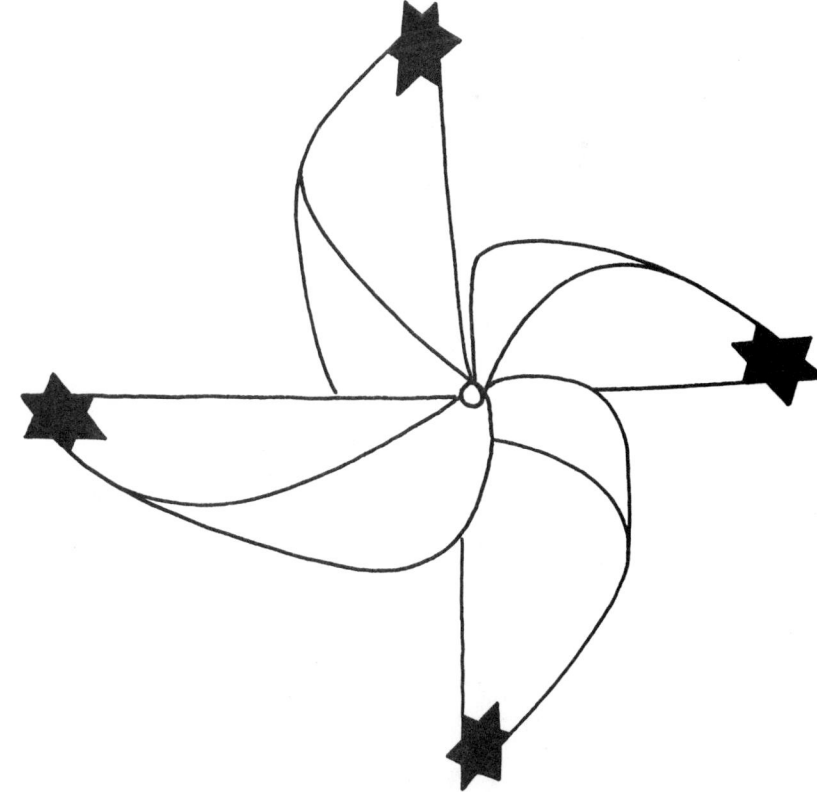

Fast, Clean & Cheap

Magen David Streamers

Materials needed: crepe paper streamers (blue and white)
paper in white and shades of blue
silver, gold and blue metallic papers
scissors
paste
stapler

Give each child a 5-foot length of blue or white crepe paper streamer. Make sure it is fireproof. Put out a selection of papers, keeping to a limited color palette for the richest effect, but providing various textures and finishes, including metallics. Then have students cut triangles from the various papers and show them how to make Star of David by pasting two of the triangles together. STAPLE the stars to the streamers—glue will dissolve the crepe paper. The resulting decorative streamer will be greater than the sum of its parts.

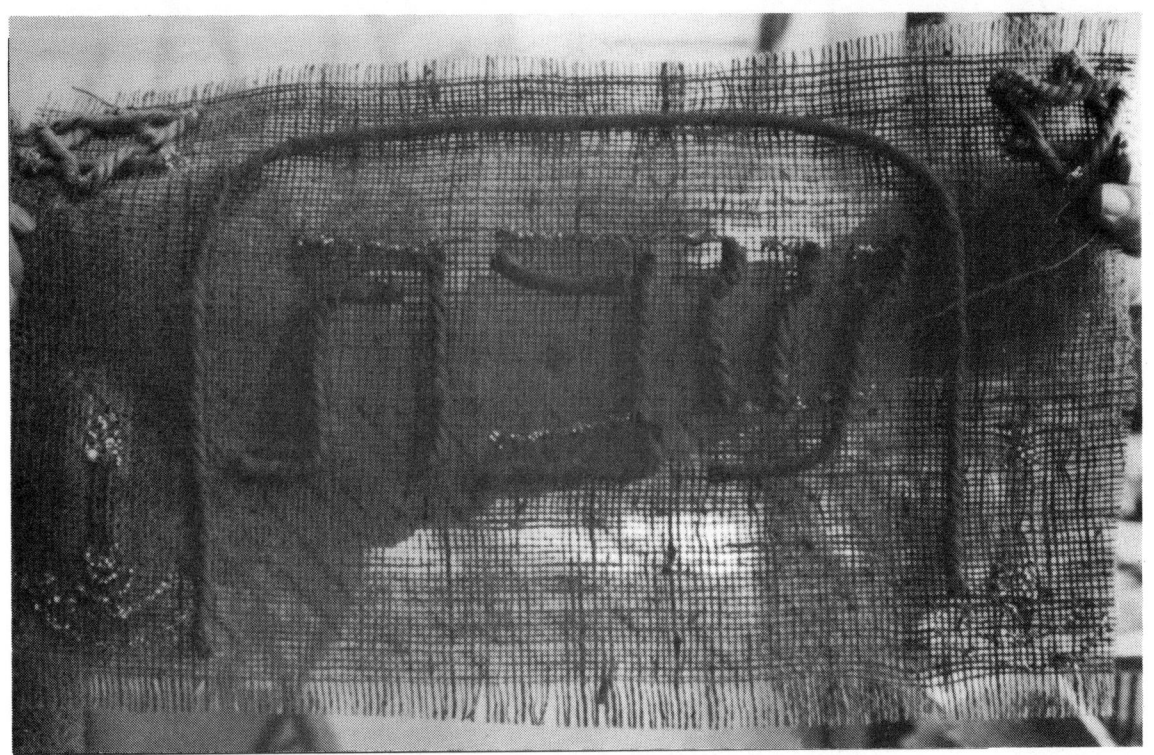

Shabbat Mats

Materials needed: burlap
fabric crayons (or regular crayons)
braid, ribbon, felt scraps, etc.
scissors

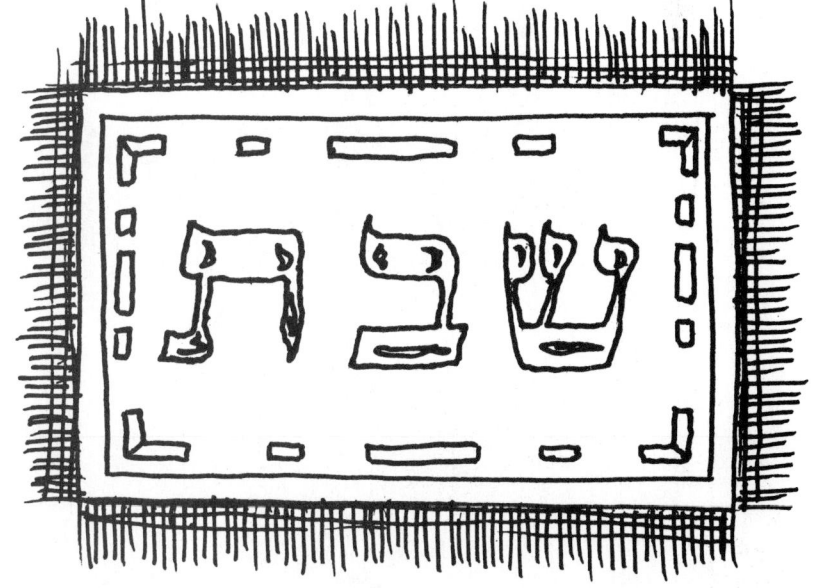

Burlap can be used to make beautiful, decorative, and inexpensive table mats for Shabbat and the holidays. It is sold in several colors. Because burlap is usually sold in 36" widths, you should cut mats about 12" x 18" to get 6 mats per yard with no waste. Do nothing with the cut edges—instead, allow students to fringe them. Five- and six-year-olds can do this and it gives the mat an elegant, professional finish. The center of the mat can be stencilled with the word "Shabbat" (or "Pesah", etc.). Then the rest of the mat can be decorated with whatever materials you choose. These become family heirlooms.

Fast, Clean & Cheap

Greeting (New Year's) Cards

Sending greeting cards at Rosh Hashanah is a venerable Jewish tradition. In recent years, some people have also begun to send such greetings at other holidays, particularly Hanukkah and Passover. The following card ideas could be adapted for any of these occasions, as well as for a bar or bat mitzvah, confirmation, or any other celebration.

1) French Fold Card

#1

#2

#3

Spatter, stencil, sponge paint or print a 9" x 12" sheet of paper. When dry, fold paper in half—then in half again in the opposite direction. This is the "French fold" seen in many greeting cards. Although only one side is printed, the illusion is created that all sides of the paper are printed. After folding, exposed surfaces can be drawn upon, text added, etc.

Fast, Clean & Cheap

2) Folded Three-D Star Card

Materials needed: construction paper, 9" x 12"
scissors

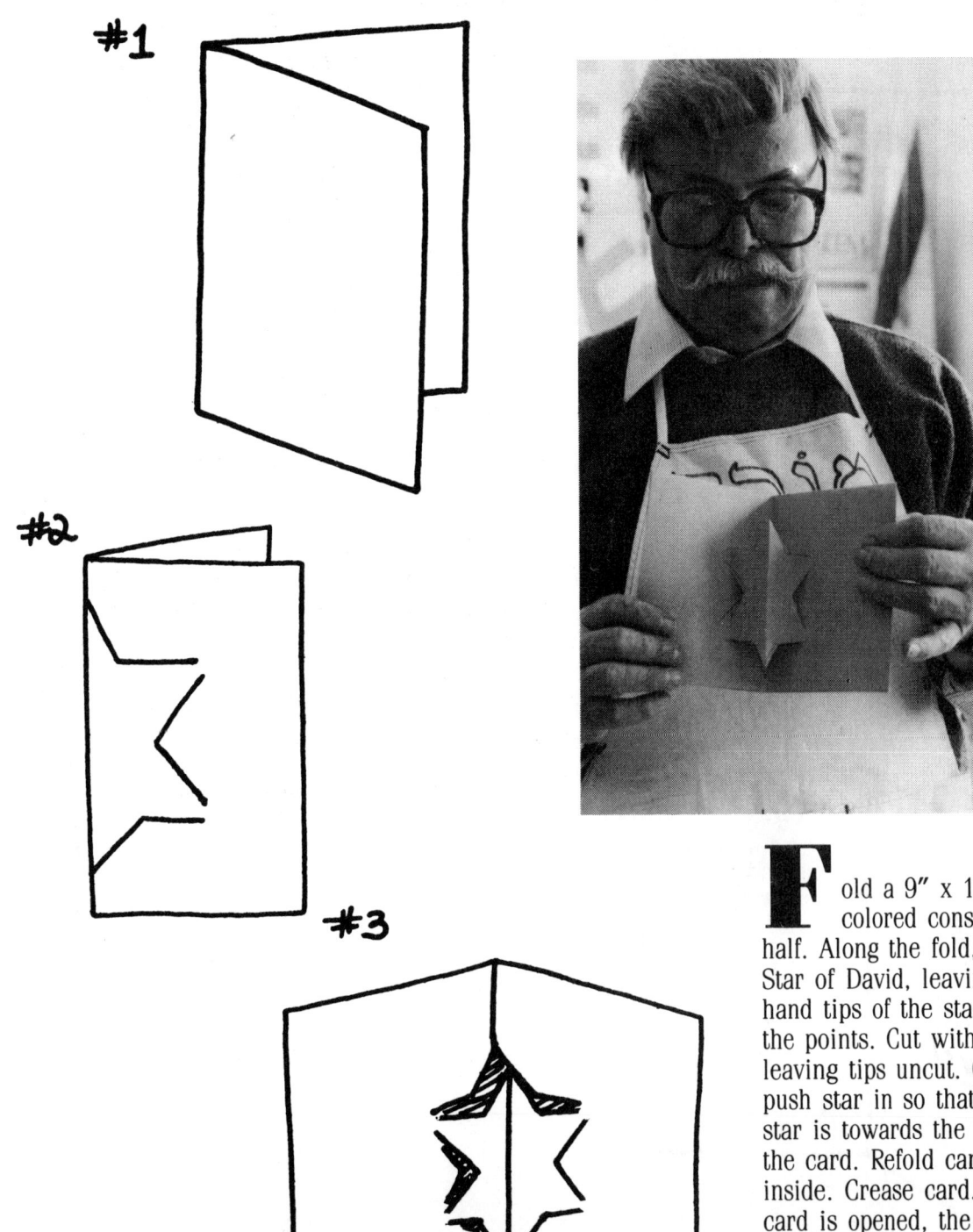

Fold a 9" x 12" piece of colored construction paper in half. Along the fold, draw half of a Star of David, leaving the two right hand tips of the star unconnected at the points. Cut with a mat knife, leaving tips uncut. Open card and push star in so that folded edge of star is towards the right-hand edge of the card. Refold card, easing star inside. Crease card. Now, when the card is opened, the star will be three-dimensional. This technique can be used with any symmetrical figure—e.g. dreidel, Torah, menorah, etc.

Fast, Clean & Cheap

3) Ark and Torah Card

Materials needed: construction paper or other stiff paper
scissors
crayons, markers or colored pencils

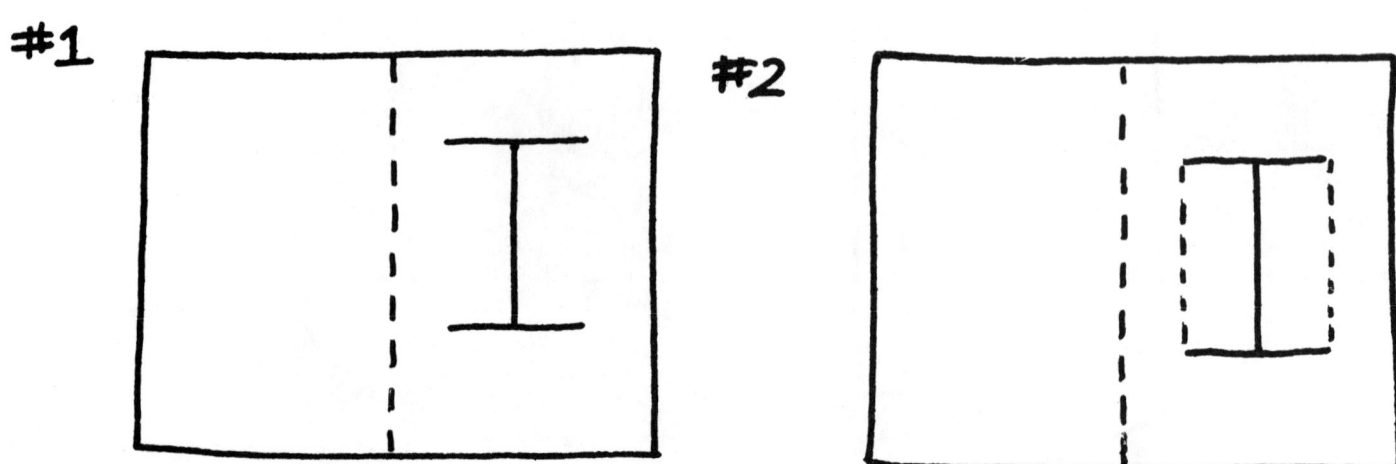

Fold paper in half. Reopen. With mat knife, cut an "I"-shaped opening in the half of the card that will be the front of the finished card, as in the illustration.

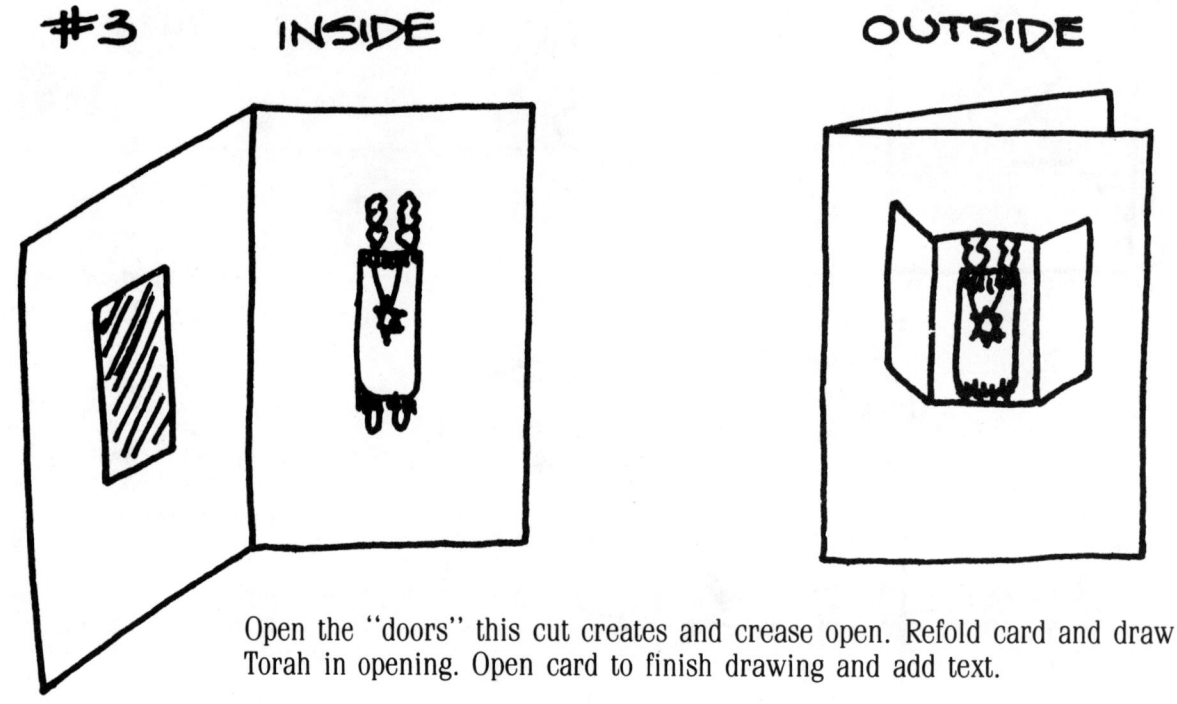

Open the "doors" this cut creates and crease open. Refold card and draw Torah in opening. Open card to finish drawing and add text.

4) Honeycomb Card

Materials needed: honeycomb paper
construction paper
scissors
glue

Honeycomb paper is an exciting new material that has recently become available. This is the kind of paper found in old-fashioned cards that fanned out into a three-dimensional shape when the card was opened. It is basically several layers of tissue paper held together by glue lines. The paper comes in large sheets (about 20" x 36") but can be cut into small pieces, perhaps 2" x 4" for this project, so that it is actually quite economical per project, even though a sheet of it is expensive. Currently, honeycomb paper is available in white only.

To use the paper in making a card, draw any *symmetrical* religious shape, and then trace *half* of the design onto the honeycomb paper, keeping the glue lines horizontal. Cut out this design. Then, fold a piece of construction paper in half for the card. Paste or glue the honeycomb paper design into the crease, being sure to attach *both sides* of the honeycomb paper to the card.

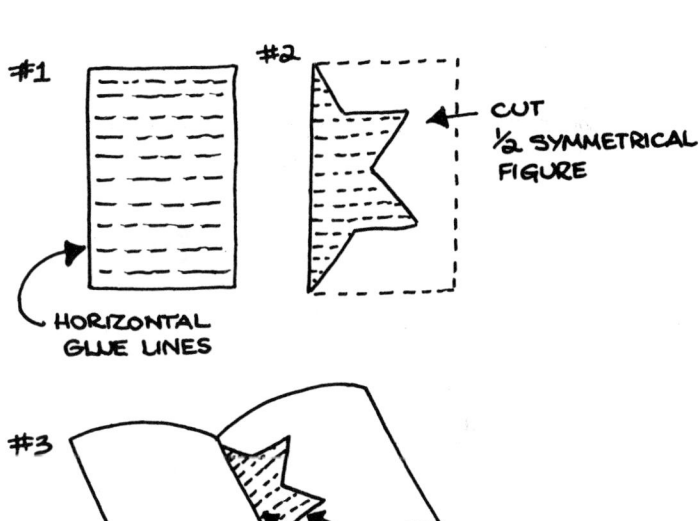

Close the card and press the whole thing together. After glue or paste is thoroughly dry, open the card. In the center, your three-dimensional design will appear—very professional and exciting!

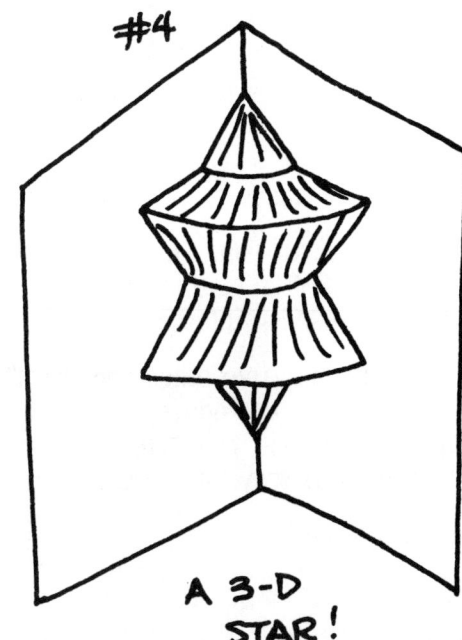

Fast, Clean & Cheap

SOME COSTUME ACCESSORIES

Every year the Jewish school has a major costuming extravaganza for Purim, but in addition, costumes can enliven plays and skits for school assemblies, and even enrich classroom role-plays. Biblical costume, luckily, can be effectively created from sheets, towels and bathrobes for the most part, with just a little help from accessories like those that follow.

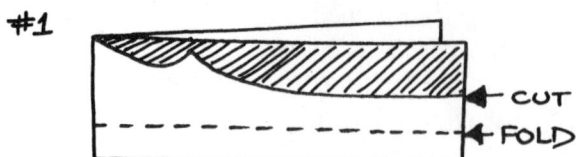

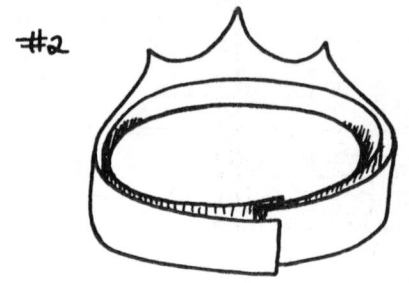

1) Crown

Materials needed: construction paper strip, 6" x 24"
stapler
scissors
sequins, glitter, markers, etc. (for decorating)

Fold paper strip in half as in the illustration. Cut crown this way and you will have a symmetrical design. After cutting, open paper and fold up on dotted line. This will give needed reinforcement to the headband.

Tuck one end of crown (about 5 inches) into other end. GENTLY try crown on head of student, pushing down to adjust size. When crown fits, carefully remove and staple. This will result in a custom-fitted crown for each student. Decorate with crayons, markers, glitter, sequins, feathers, etc.

Fast, Clean & Cheap

2) Paper Domino Mask

Materials needed: construction paper, 9" x 12"
mat knife
sequins, markers, etc. (for decoration)
tape

Fold 9" x 12" construction paper lengthwise. Using a mat knife, cut out shaded area of illustration. Four or five masks may be cut at one time with a sharp mat knife. Do cutting on a stack of newspapers. Open paper and roll bottom half as shown. Tape rolls together. Now, the mask may be decorated with crayons, markers, sequins, glitter, feathers, etc. You now have a domino mask on a support, without the danger of a stick. This is a safe mask for little children.

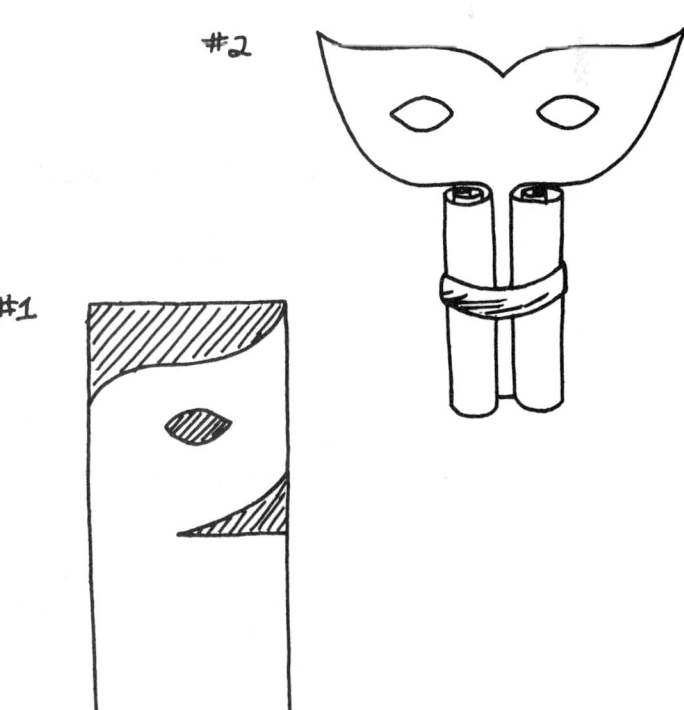

Fast, Clean & Cheap

3) Paper Bag Mask

Materials needed: #10 paper bag
scissors
scraps of fabric, yarn, colored paper
crayons or markers

Be sure bag is large enough to cover a child's head. With bag folded, cut as in #1. Open bag. TEACHER should cut openings for eyes. Let students add ears, nose, mane, and other features with colored papers, cloth scraps, yarns, etc.

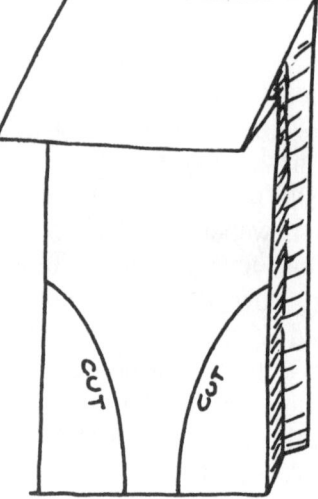

#1

Fast, Clean & Cheap

4) Egg Carton Mask

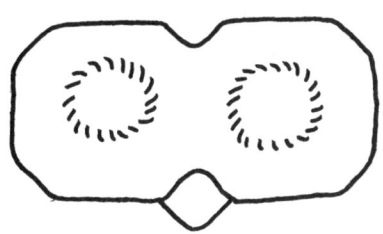

Materials needed: foam egg carton
scissors
elastic cord
scraps of fabric, yarn, paper, leather, etc.

A good mask foundation can be made from a foam egg carton. Cut carton so that you have two adjacent egg hollows and the spacer in between to serve as the nose. A one dozen carton will yield 5 such shapes. This is just the foundation. Tissue paper veils or construction paper details can be glued on; cloth, flowers, sequins, feathers, etc. can be added for decoration. There is no limit to the creativity that will be generated. The teacher can cut out eye-holes and fasten an elastic cord for wearing.

Fast, Clean & Cheap

5) Three-Cornered Hat

Materials needed: construction paper strip 4" x 24"
construction paper 9" x 12"
scissors
stapler

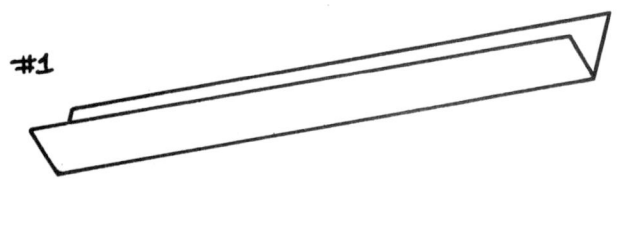
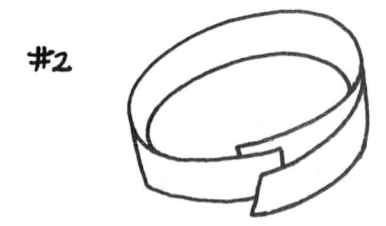
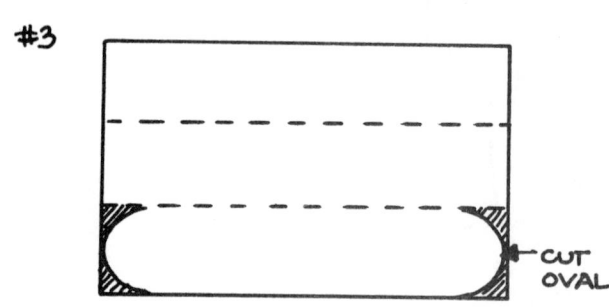
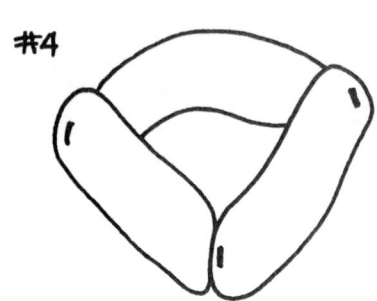
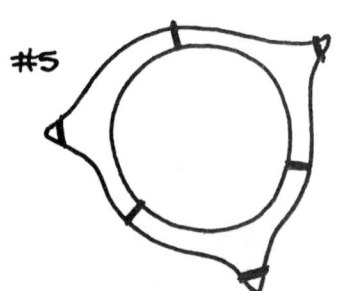

Fold the 4" x 24" paper strip in half lengthwise. Overlap about 4 inches and try on student to get correct head size. Staple. Fold the 9" x 12" inch piece of paper lengthwise into thirds. Cut the largest oval possible, cutting all three at the same time. Staple 3 ovals at the ends. Slip over headband and staple. Not only is this a good Haman's hat, but it is also a good tricorn for patriotic historical figures.

Purim Gragger

Materials needed: thin, cheap paper plate
dried beans
stapler
crayons, markers, ribbon (for decoration)

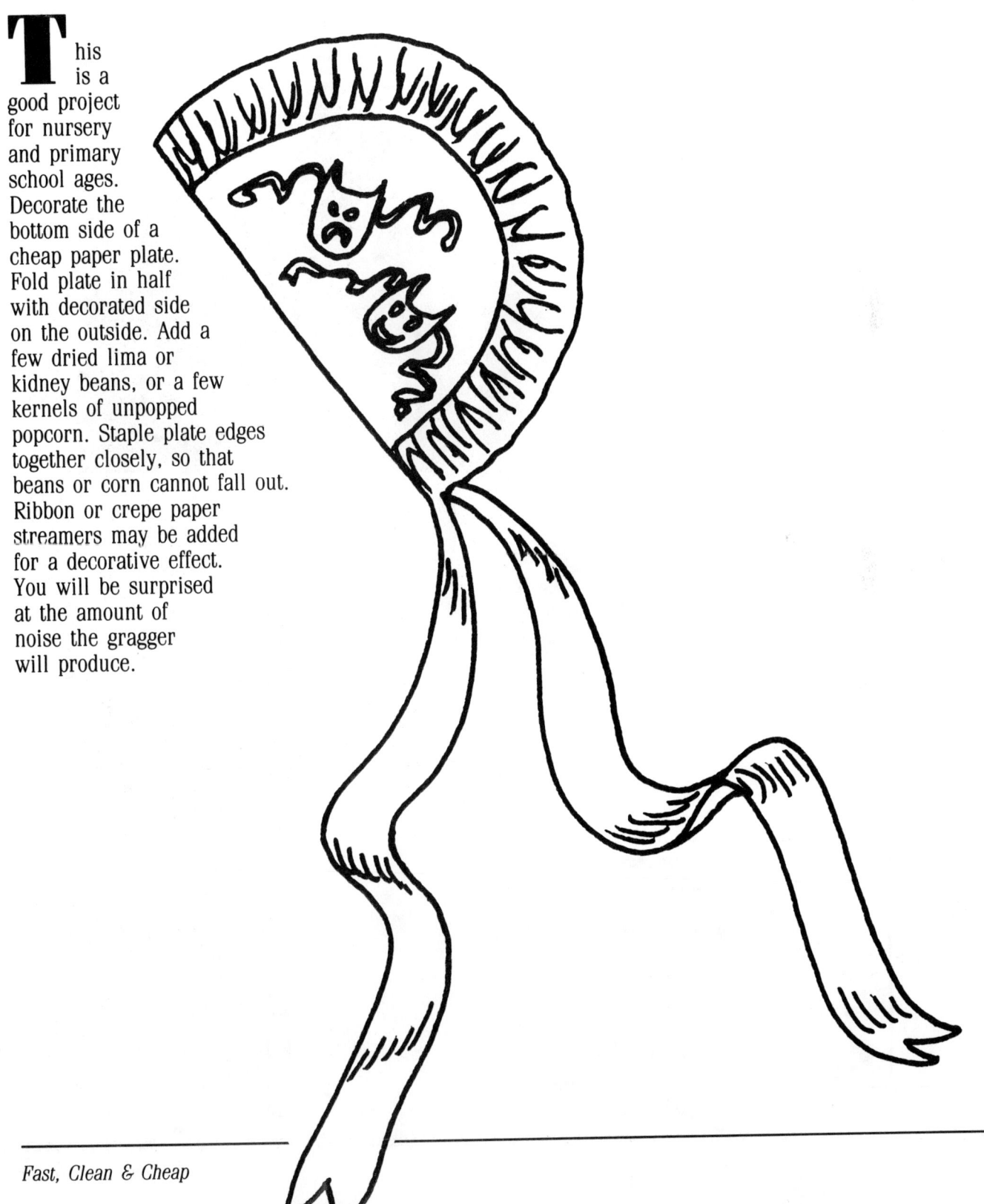

This is a good project for nursery and primary school ages. Decorate the bottom side of a cheap paper plate. Fold plate in half with decorated side on the outside. Add a few dried lima or kidney beans, or a few kernels of unpopped popcorn. Staple plate edges together closely, so that beans or corn cannot fall out. Ribbon or crepe paper streamers may be added for a decorative effect. You will be surprised at the amount of noise the gragger will produce.

Fast, Clean & Cheap

Stencilled Paper Israeli Flag

Materials needed: tagboard, 12" x 18"
mat knife
white drawing or construction paper, 12" x 18"
silver, gold or blue spray paint
tape

Using the tagboard, cut a stencil like the one in the illustration, using a sharp mat knife. Place stencil over white paper and LIGHTLY spray, with spray paint. Silver and gold spray paint have the least residue, although you may choose to use blue for this particular project because of the colors of the Israeli flag. Then cut paper apart on dotted line, and you will have two flags with no waste. Roll large end as in illustration and tape. Here is a stickless flag that is safe for any child. This flag is adaptable for other purposes besides Israeli Independence Day.

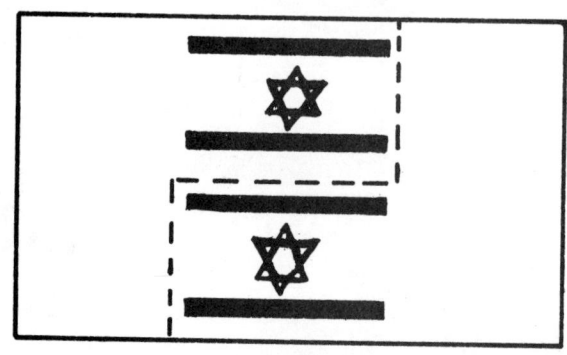

Fast, Clean & Cheap

Lacing Card Israeli Flag

Materials needed:
 tagboard, 9" x 12"
 one or two packages 9" x 12" construction paper (white)
 electric drill
 blue yarn
 cellulose tape

Make pattern at right on 9" x 12" tagboard. Tape pattern to one or two full packs of white construction paper. Working on a scrap block of wood, DRILL the holes in the pattern with an electric hand drill. A 1/4 inch drill will work fine. This little bit of preparation will result in 50 to 100 worksheets. Students can lace with yarn whose ends are wrapped with cellulose tape for ease in lacing.

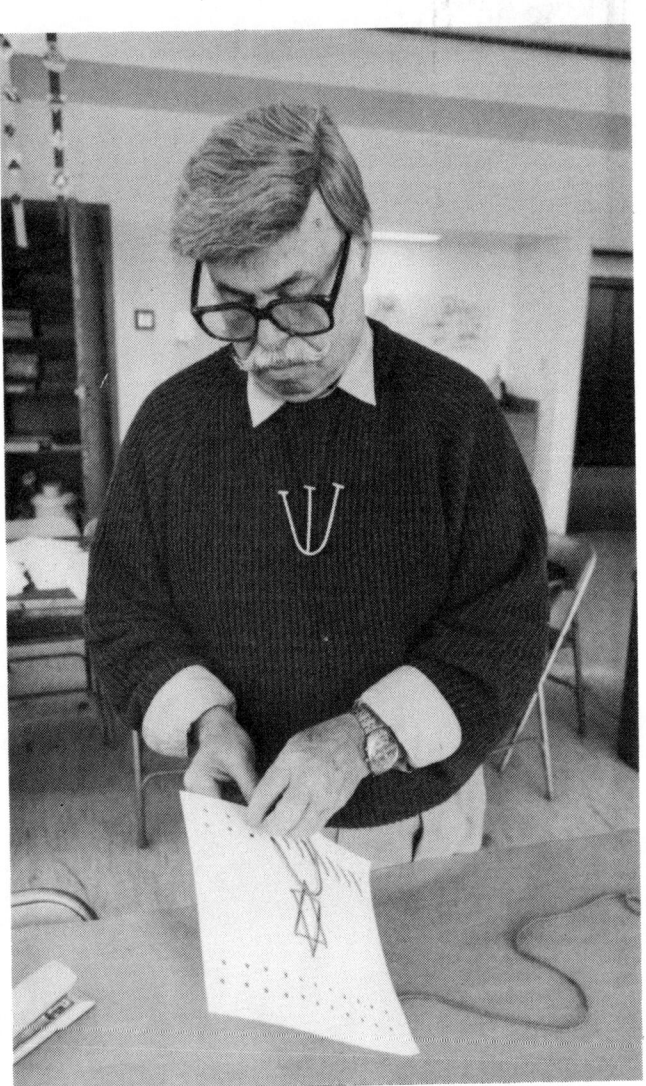

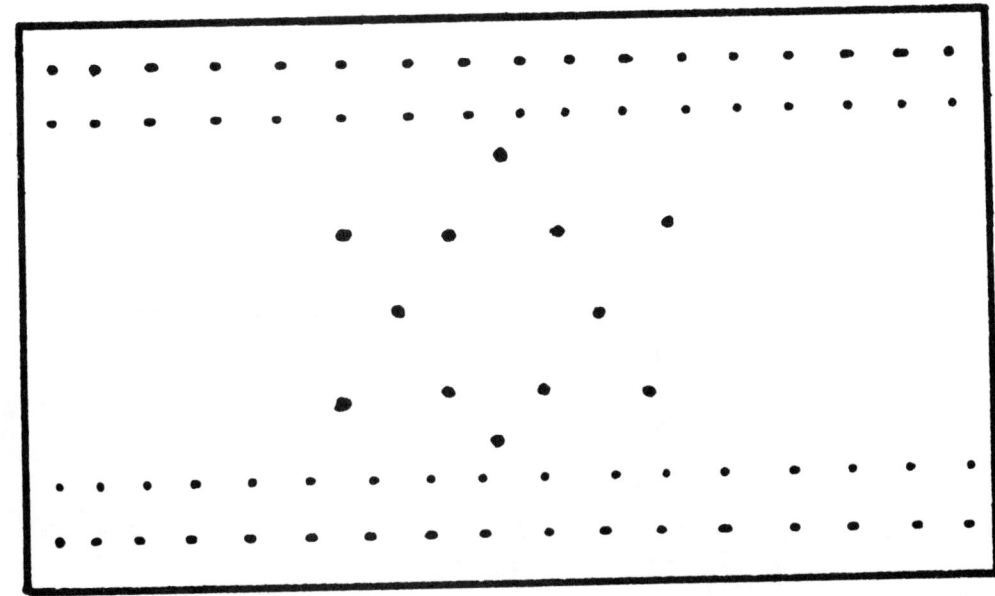

Fast, Clean & Cheap

FLOWERS

Flowers are cheerful decorations for almost any occasion, and in the Jewish school they are particularly appropriate for the harvest festivals of Sukkot and Shavuot, as well as for Tu Bish'vat. Two kinds appear below, and a third type is described earlier in the book in the section on ORIGAMI (PAPER FOLDING).

Tissue Paper Flowers

Materials needed: colored tissue paper, 12" x 18"
pipe cleaners

Large flowers can be easily made by finely pleating 2 or 3 sheets of 12" x 18" tissue together. Pinch together at arrow, and tie with a pipe cleaner. Gently separate tissue at edges, which will result in a cup-like form—like a large cabbage rose. Colors can be solid, shaded or intermixed. These are great for decorations and/or bulletin boards.

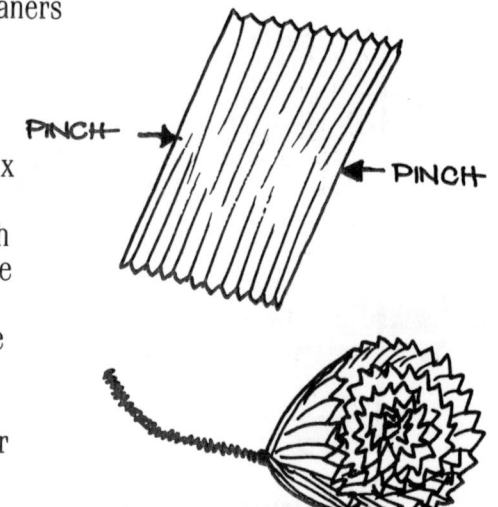

Fast, Clean & Cheap

Simple Flower Bouquet

Materials needed: colored tissue paper scraps
3 long pipe cleaners, preferably green
large empty thread spool
scissors

#1

#2

#3

#4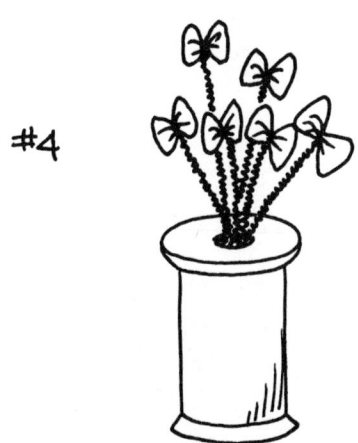

Cut 2-inch squares of many colors of tissue paper. Twist tissue. Using long pipe cleaners, fasten a twist at each end. Fold pipe cleaner roughly in half and insert in an empty spool. Two or three such pipe cleaners make a good bouquet.
Five-year-olds can do this easily.

Fast, Clean & Cheap

Flower Basket

Materials needed: construction paper, 9" x 12"
scissors
paste
stapler

A VERY simple flower basket (for a May basket, or Mother's Day) can be made from one sheet of 9" x 12" paper. Cut a 3" x 9" strip off the end for the handle. The remaining 9-inch square is all that is needed for the basket.

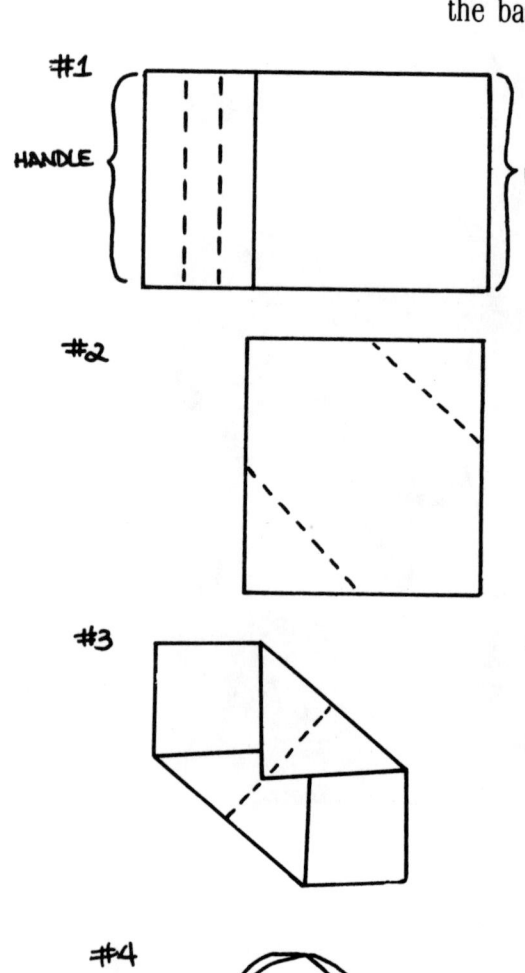

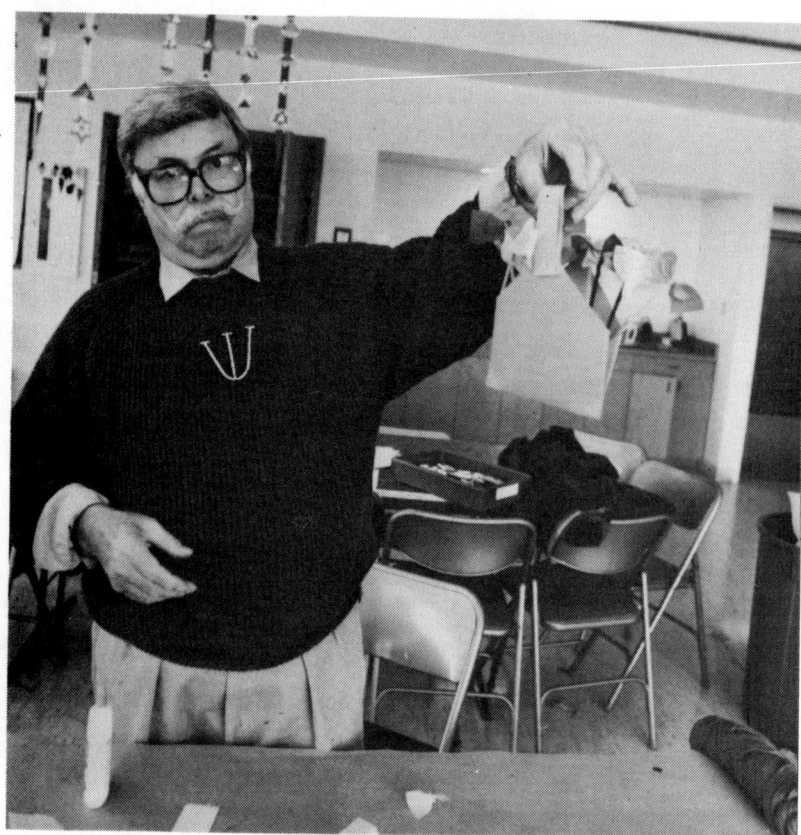

Fold the 3" x 9" strip lengthwise in thirds. This is the handle. Fold opposite diagonal corners of the remaining square as in the diagram. Paste down the overlapping corners. Then fold on dotted line. Glue or staple protruding corners to handle ends. Fill with real or paper flowers. This basket could also be used for Mishloah Manot if the food to be delivered as Purim gifts were small and lightweight enough.

Refrigerator Magnets

Materials needed: heavyweight felt, various colors
casein (white) glue
self-adhesive magnetic strips (2" per project)
scissors

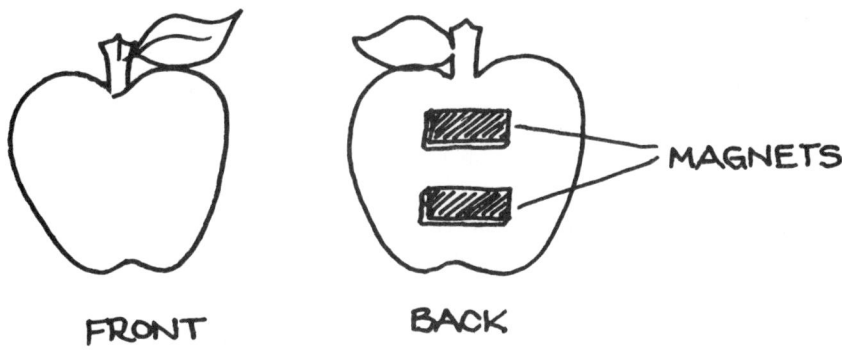

FRONT   BACK

This is a project that can serve many ages in the religious school. The basic material is felt. Try to get the heaviest weight possible. Give out 3-inch squares to minimize waste. The smaller scraps created when students cut out the basic shapes they want can then be cut up and used as embellishments. Scrap yarns can also be used. Use casein (white) glue. Paste will *NOT* work. The casein glue dries virtually colorless. Adhesive magnetic strips can be bought by the foot. About two inches of the magnetic strip per unit is sufficient. Two one-inch pieces, spaced apart, will cling to a metal surface better than one two-inch strip. Felt pieces can be cut in any shapes, relating to any holiday or subject. Fruits and vegetables for Sukkot are popular items. Markers can be used to delineate details.

Fast, Clean & Cheap

Paper Ḥanukkah Latern

Materials needed: construction paper, 9" x 12" (white or light blue)
scissors
paste or stapler
gummed foil stars (optional)

Paper Hanukkah lanterns are a good classroom decorative project and are easily made. Use white or light blue 9" x 12" construction paper. Fold in half horizontally. Cut off one inch at the end for later use as a handle. Then cut from the folded edge to about one inch from the free edges of the paper, making cuts about 3/4 inch apart. Open fold—form into a cylinder, and paste or staple together. Use the one-inch strip for a handle. Foil stars can be added for sparkle.

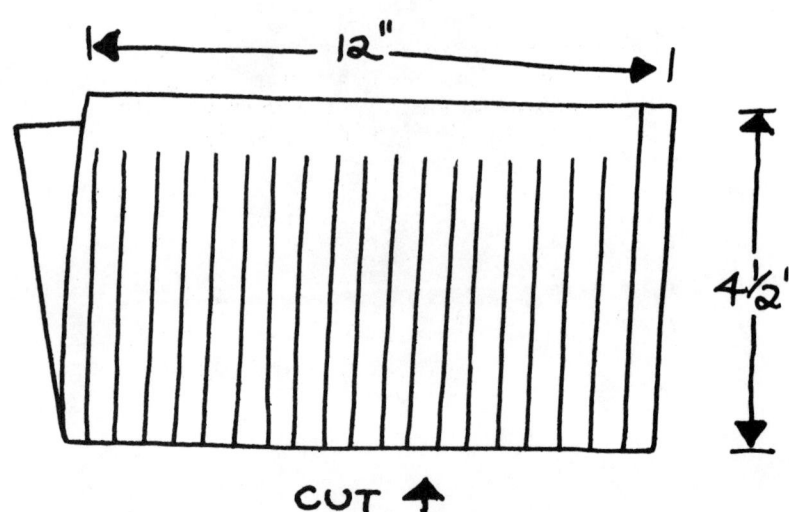

Fast, Clean & Cheap

Wooden Ḥanukkiah

Materials needed: 10-inch section of a 2" x 4" board
aluminum foil
cotton rug warp or other heavy cord
glue
drill with 3/8" bit

A usable (and reusable) Hanukkah menorah can be made from a board this way. Stand the 10-inch board on edge and drill nine evenly-spaced holes in the top edge. The diameter of the holes should be 3/8" to hold regular Hanukkah candles. On the larger flat surface of the board, make a menorah pattern of rug warp or other heavy cord or string and glue to the board. Then cover the wooden block with a piece of aluminum foil. Using your fingers, mold the foil around the menorah design. The foil will stretch slightly and the design will appear in relief. Use a candle to poke through the foil to open the previously drilled holes on the top edge. This is a menorah that can be used year after year.

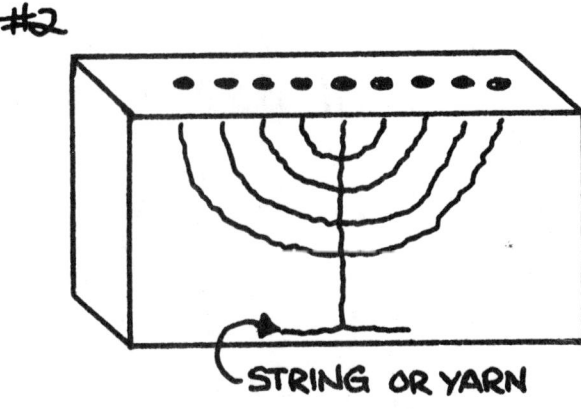

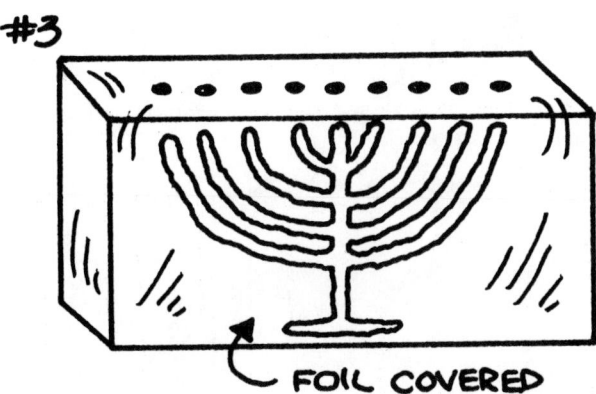

Fast, Clean & Cheap

Judaic Memory Box

Materials needed: empty "nostalgia" or "memory" box
variety of construction materials (toothpicks, yarn, foil, paper, beads, cloth, etc.)
fancy papers, wallpaper scraps or old greeting cards (for backgrounds)

Many art or framing stores sell small compartmented "memory" boxes that are ideal for this project. They are cheapest if bought unassembled. After assembling boxes, let students make miniature bits of Judaica that have meaning for them to place in the various compartments. Items that can be made might include a tallit, a kiddush cup, a Torah, a Magen David, candlesticks, etc. Pipe cleaners are an excellent medium. It is especially effective to use wallpaper scraps, old greeting cards or fancy papers to line the different compartments before placing objects in them.

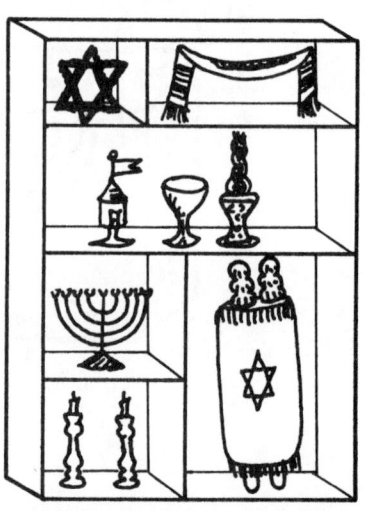

Glossary

CASEIN GLUE—glue made from milk products; water soluble until dried. Also known as "white glue". Trade names—Elmer's, Borden's

CELLULOSE TAPE—usually, a clear plastic sticky tape. Good for a one-time application only. Trade name—Scotch tape

CONTOUR DRAWING—a line drawn around a form, echoing that form.

COLLAGE—an assemblage of materials pasted together from the French verb, *coller*, to paste.

DUCTILITY—a metal's ability to be drawn out or stretched.

GAUGE—a measure of the thickness of sheet metals. Metal less than 1/8 inch thick is usually measured by gauge. The higher the number, the thinner the metal. "8 gauge" metal is 1/8 inch thick.

KIPPAH—head covering worn by pious Jews, also called "yarmulke"

LIVER OF SULPHUR—a sulphur compound which has the ability to darken or oxidize copper or silver.

LULAV—palm branch bound together with myrtle and willow twigs, used on Sukkot.

MALLEABILITY—formable, bendable quality of some metals.

MASKING TAPE—a crinkly sticky paper tape that gives with the humidity. Usually can be repositioned.

MEZUZAH—Decorative case hung at an entrance to a room, containing a prayer on a parchment scroll.

MIZRAH—plaque placed on a wall to indicate the direction one must face in order to turn toward Jerusalem in prayer.

MOEBIUS STRIP—a strip of paper twisted once or twice and then joined at the ends to form a ring.

OIL CRAYONS—brilliant chalks with an oil base. Trade name—CRAYPAS

ORIGAMI—Japanese art of intricate paper folding to create three-dimensional objects. Very involved. Seldom uses glue.

REPOUSSE—Formed in relief. Usually pushed out from the back.

OIL CLAYS—plastic modeling clays, using oil rather than water as a vehicle. Practically never dries out. Trade names—Plasticene, Permaplast

SYMMETRICAL—designed so that one side of a central axis is a mirror image of the other side.

WHITE GLUE—see CASEIN GLUE.

Art Material Sources

NASCO West
1524 Princeton Ave.
Modesto, CA 95352
(209) 529-6957

California Crafts Supply
1096 North Main St.
Orange, CA 92667
(714) 633-8891

Triarco/Arts & Crafts, Inc.
14650 28th Ave. North
Plymouth, MN 55441
(612) 559-5590

Valley School Suppliers, Inc.
P.O. Box 1579
Appleton, WI 54911
(414) 734-5712

NASCO House of Crafts
901 Janesville Road
Fort Atkinson, WI 52538
(414) 563-2446

Sax Arts & Crafts
P.O. Box 2002
Milwaukee, WI 53202
(414) 272-4900

Economy Handicrafts
50-21 69th Street
Woodside, New York 11377-7598
(718) 426-1600

This list is not meant as an endorsement of the above mentioned firms, but merely as a sample listing. Most firms charge $3-$4 for a catalog but will send one free if requested on school stationary.

Additional Projects

Additional Projects

Additional Projects

Additional Projects

Additional Projects

Additional Projects